Everything You Need To Know About The Three Bees:

- **BOOKS**
- **BEERS**
- **BABES**

Published by National Lampoon Press

National Lampoon, Inc. • 8228 Sunset Boulevard • Los Angeles • CA 90046 • USA • AMEX:NLN

NATIONAL LAMPOON, NATIONAL LAMPOON PRESS and colophon are trademarks of National Lampoon

Van Wilder Guide To Graduating College In Eight Years Or More: Written and edited by MoDMaN
Additional Material:
A Word From Brock Spady YouTube Star by Brock Spady
National Party School Ranking According To Miiiiiatch by Mitch Higgins
The Van Wilder Files by Mason Brown, Joe Osterlee, Sean Crespo, Steve Brykman

p. cm.

ISBN-10: 0978832337
ISBN-13: 978-0978832339
$12.95 U.S. - $15.95 Canada

Book Design and Production by
JK NAUGHTON

Art Direction and Illustration by
MoDMaN

Van Wilder Files Illustration by
Joe Osterlee

 is a registered trademark of The Thirdbrand and www.thethirdbrand.com

1 3 5 7 9 10 8 6 4 2

APRIL 2007

WWW.NATIONALLAMPOON.COM

NATIONAL LAMPOON

VAN WILDER

Guide To Graduating

COLLEGE

IN EIGHT YEARS OR MORE

MoDMaN

Editorial Assistance, and Additional Material by
Brock Spady, Mitch Higgins

Material adapted from National Lampoon Dotcom by
Mason Brown, Joe Osterlee, Sean Crespo, Steve Brykman

Survey Of College Students by
Tracy Caldwell

Some story elements and characters in this book were derived from the
original screenplay, National Lampoon's Van Wilder by
Brent Goldberg, and David Wagner

A WORD

THAT'S ABOUT IT

THIS IS IT

Don't Treat Every Situation Like It's Life And Death Because You'll Die... A Lot Of Times

On a clear blue morning as the spring semester of my third senior year was beginning, I found myself gazing out across the campus of Coolidge College. My rooftop vantage afforded me a panorama of rolling lawns and tree-lined walks still in winter's slumber but awakening to the promise of the warming sun soon to come. I'll always remember that day. I think it was a Tuesday.

WE'VE GOT A JUMPER

Suddenly my reverie was shattered as a shout pierced the morning air.... "We've got a jumper!" As I approached the scared and nervous youth, his chin quivering, and snot oozing from a reddened nose, I wondered how could I have not noticed him on the stone edifice of the very rooftop I shared with him. Then I realized Timmy's true despair. He was invisible. He'd missed all of the wonder, excitement, and camaraderie of the college life. It'd passed him by and left him convinced that no one cared, that no one understood.

But I did understand. Call me nuts but I believed in Timmy. I spent a good five or six minutes talking that boy down. And the more I talked with Timmy, informing him of all the joys and treasures his new life as a Coolidge underclassman would bring, he seemed to get increasingly agitated, mumbling something about his name not being Timmy.

Knowing my cool demeanor would soothe his fractured nerves I gazed skyward wistfully continuing my pontification...

******

Timmy jumped.

******

VanWilderism #110
Never sleep with anyone crazier than yourself.
Write that down.

There was so much I wanted to share with Timmy. There was so much knowledge of the university culture culled from my seven years of enrollment to enlighten him with. Luckily for Timmy, a rescue squad had time to maneuver a safety net below and caught him before his brains were dashed on the pavement. Not long after, I heard from his girlfriend Sally that Timmy swore he never wanted to experience anything like that again.

******

Did I mention I wasn't wearing pants at the time?

******

Timmy, Sally, I dedicate this book to you. I hope it helps and remember my credo... Don't be a fool. Stay in school.

Van Wilder

GETTING IN

Procrastination Is An Immovable Force Of Nature

Congratulations Timmy, you've embarked on the spring semester of the rest of your life. You are going to college and it's time to say so long to the 'rents and hello to a few new student bodies. You've made an excellent decision to kick-off your collegiate experience with the purchase of the *Van Wilder Guide To Graduating College In Eight Years Or More.*

I'm going to assume that there were several compelling reasons why you selected this guide as a scholastic work belt for your educational tools, but I'll bet the title had something to do with it. Let's examine that for a quick one, okay Timmy? The most important and operative word in the title is "Graduate." You want to finish what you start, right sport? Get a leg-up on the competition, be recognized as an achiever, and more than likely because getting this college thing done properly means there'll be copious amounts of cheddar in your immediate future.

That's great, graduating is a good objective and these are all excellent reasons for heading out on an exploration of the university universe. So let's take a look at the secondary imperative in the title "*...In Eight Years Or More.*" Listen, it took me seven years to complete my studies and since I've been a graduate for a few years now, I can look back and honestly say...

LUNCHTIME

VanWilderism #35
Ambivalence is the mother of inertia.
Write that down.

Wow! I probably could have milked an extra spin or two out of the college calendar.

Now some people might take a dim view of turning a four-year scholastic schedule into what you might refer to as a protracted passion. They might even claim that this is an example of gross procrastination. Here's a concept I'd like to introduce you to:

******

Procrastination is not a bad habit.

******

Joseph R. Ferrari:
An associate professor of psychology stated, "Telling someone who procrastinates to get a weekly planner is like telling someone with chronic depression to just cheer up."
The Chronicle of Higher Education, 2002

Oh sure, there are academicians who'd prefer to treat procrastination as a four letter word. Like, what are they thinking? Maybe: "ocra" or "asti"? That's just silly – crazy academics and their fancy vocabulary.

You may be surprised to learn this, but you, Timmy, as a college student, are the subject of many scientific studies. And in this case everyone studying you wants to find the cure for procrastination. Procrastination, which these studies define as the act of delaying responsible decisions, is basically the lack of checks on the old "to-do" list. That is, if you ever got around to doing a "to-do" list.

There are very lofty discussions within these studies deliberating whether procrastination is biological, in which case you've got serious issues with your prefrontal lobe cortex, or whether it's psychological, meaning you've got a hell of a tumbling run worked out for the mental gymnastics gold medal round.

But the funny thing is, the studies conclude that everyone is a procrastinator. It's just a matter of degree. According to a noted psychologist, 90% of all college students are habitual procrastinators, and 25% are chronic. So, does that mean the best and brightest our great country has to offer are either brain damaged or whacko? Whoa-ho there, I'm not going to stand here and let anyone run down the fine college students of the U.S. of A. And I don't know about you but I don't feel brain damaged; well there was that episode during the Jäger Olympics but that's not important right now.

You know, if I had to sum up the reasons why you selected this book, I'm going to go all in and say it's because we're going to deal with how things really are. We're not going to get bogged down in what your parents, or professors, or academic studies, or focus groups happen to think about "you," or about what they think "you should do." We're going to concentrate on, "what is." Whoa, that's existential.

Note: If you haven't taken Philosophy 101 yet, I recommend the course – very enlightening.

The thing to remember about procrastination is this: out of the 25% of college students that are chronic procrastinators there's going to be a lot of them who will end up failing out of school. And you don't have to be Professor Brainiac to know that a "one-semester-and-out" program is not going to yield eight years of academic fulfillment.

Don't get me wrong, if your idea of the preferred college experience is: show up for a semester, blow off all your classes except for co-ed beach volleyball and then sober up just in time to receive notice that the university has concluded that you're an academic liability, then that's okay. Seriously, there's nothing wrong with that, champ. I'm not here to pass judgment. You'll get plenty of that from Mom and Dad, and I don't even want to think about the look you'll get from Nana at Christmas time. If you are going to go that route though, you should at least be honest with yourself and admit that that's what you're doing. Oh, and please no tears when Moms is at the curb with the family minivan

Procrastinate:
Originally from the Latin *procrativus*, which means I'm gonna look that up as soon as I get a chance.

to take you back home to live in the basement and Uncle Bobby calls to let you know he's pulled some strings to get your old job back at the Maxi-Mart. Reminds me of my first roommate, Rex. He spent the entire first quarter of my first freshman year just sitting around drinking Jack Daniels all day and playing guitar. Girls really dug that guy... big time rock star now... but I know deep down he's just half the man he could have become... very hollow inside... really sad... really, really sad.

VanWilderism #12
Persistence is omnipotent.
Write that down.

Even if you learn nothing else from the *Van Wilder Guide To Graduating College In Eight Years Or More*, the biggest idea you'll be presented with, and quite possibly the key to your success in school and a great life lesson, is not going to be a statistical analysis of your and your peers' procrastinatory practices. No, no, no. Pack your bags Timmy, you're moving to Flow Town.

******

But what's Flow Town, Mr. Wilder?

*****

Please, call me Van. I'm not the president or mayor of Flow Town, but I do have a sweet little condo over on Main Street so I'm prepared to clue you in. But listen Sally, this isn't necessarily going to be an easy concept to grasp, so pay attention and I'll try to keep it simple. I know this may be hard to believe, but I was not always the pillar of practical patronage that I am today. It's true I was a mess until I was acquainted with the idea of Flow Town some time around mid-term in the fall of my second sophomore year. I hope this helps you as much as it did me.

Here are the only laws of Flow Town.

1. If you think about eating your lunch, you will.
2. Even when the cameras are on, don't go big unless you're ready.
3. Just because it's boring doesn't mean it's good for you.
4. Live your own reality.

The First Law of Flow Town, "If you think about eating your lunch, you will," means you are your decisions. If you choose to dwell on success rather than obsessing about disaster then chances are you'll be successful – and a lot more fun on road trips.

The Second Law of Flow Town states, "Even when the cameras are on, don't go big unless you're ready." You're on a bigger stage now Sally, and if you want to perform at a higher level, dream big. But when you act on your dreams, know your limitations. In other words, if you hate math, you'll want to shy away from that nuclear physics degree program.

The Third Law of Flow Town, "Just because it's boring doesn't mean it's good for you" is self-explanatory. Just don't do it! Unless you're into self-abuse, in which case I know some pretty weird religious sects you might be interested in. Could be a good PhD program for a cultural anthropology post-grad, but it weirds me out. So, let's just leave it alone, shall we?

The Fourth Law of Flow Town is, "Live your own reality." Sounds New Age-y and queer? Okay, fine, don't say it out loud unless you're sure you're alone. Sally, Sally, Sally, jealously and envy are not attractive accessories, so leave them at home with that cheap costume jewelry and floral party dress that you thought was so "retro" when you picked it up at the Salvation Army sidewalk sale for fifty cents. Let's say your roommate or best friend rarely studies, parties all the time, never sleeps, and coasts to good grades. This doesn't mean that you need to adopt these habits or

Eating Your Lunch:
A painful and or sometimes embarrassing accident usually involving impact between the face and a resistant surface.

College Students:
were found to procrastinate more for written assignments and less for tests or examinations
Solomon and Rothblum, 1984

should punish yourself because you have to work hard. And on the flip, you don't have license to look down on them for "goofing off."

There are no overnight successes, Sally. We all have our own paths to walk – remember to stretch, you don't want to pull anything.

Flow Town's not on Google Maps yet so here's a diagram to help you locate it.

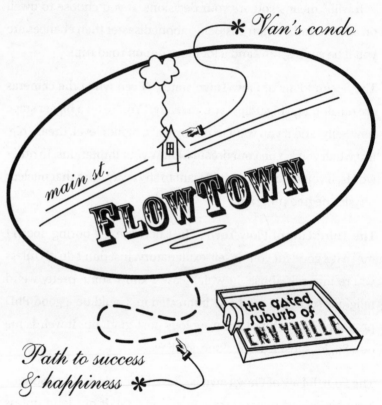

Do you think the typical "4 year college" should be longer or shorter than 4 years?
College should be forever.
– *John McCue, Senior in Neuroscience, UCLA*

Fat, Drunk And Stupid Is No Way To Go Through Life, But Dealing With Sleep Deprivation Is Mandatory

If you'd like to get an idea of what to expect from college get on a plane and fly into Newark New Jersey International, take the Manhattan Express to the Port Authority Bus Terminal. Once in the city take the transit system to Times Square. Around 5:00 p.m. find a spot on the median and stare up to find the top of the skyscrapers. Take a deep breath. Feel that? That's commerce and culture whizzing by overhead. That's the business day sprinting to the finish line. That's the theater district coming to life. That's the restaurants and bars beckoning, and the night calling in the city that never sleeps. Don't look down though; that's a homeless man pissing on your shoes.

In college you're going to get cultural, environmental, sensory, and intellectual overload, which is a great buzz. Remember when you were five and you pretended you were a whirling dervish in your parents' front lawn? It's very similar to that. You were pretty cute too, by the way.

But you're not in Kansas anymore Sally. And if you've chosen a big university like UCLA, NYU, or well... KSU, then you might as well have ingested pure adrenaline. Incidentally pure adrenaline is not an attractive party drug and not something to mess around with, especially freshman year.

XXLU:
11% of American universities are considered large campuses (10,000 plus students), but account for 51% of all college enrolment.

******

Just say "no" to ingesting pure adrenaline.

******

When you sum up all the administration, clerical, faculty, food and maintenance staff, Starbucks employees, ten to twenty thousand students, you, the cars, the buses, the bicycles, skateboards, hotels, motels, restaurants, apartments, and all the campus buildings, grounds, and stadiums, you're talking a mini-metropolis. It has its own politics, laws, police, and cultural identity. It's a Sims experiment on steroids. What will your thought bubble say? "Hey, this is all very exciting! Let's get wasted, go a week on four hours sleep and make it more confusing and fuzzy! I know – then we can take a month long mono-induced nappy nap – yeah!"

Slow your roll there, Sally. You've got plenty of time to experiment with inter-racial dating, all-night dance parties, petty theft, and all those wonderful things you've been dreaming of doing for so long. You don't have to cram it all into the first fifteen minutes. Trust me, there'll be more than enough opportunity to give your pops cause for pulmonary plumbing problems.

******

Pace yourself.

******

VanWilderism #168
Early to rise misses the prize, because sleeping-in late feels great.
Write that down.

In an ordinary day you'll be faced with a new experience or mind-blowing thought on average every five point six seconds. My advice: sleep when you're tired, feed your brain, dancing counts as exercise, and TSY – typing, speed-reading, yoga. You'll also find that sleep deprivation is the body's own goofy cocktail. It's best served in shots and not pitchers.

Selecting A College:
It's Not What You Know
But Who You Do That Counts

Who am I? Why am I here? Where am I going? Where you at? Are the voices in my head disturbing you? – Damn! You sure have a lot of questions. Try turning the Neurotic-Master 9000 down a notch or two a'right, Timmy? Stressing life's philosophical meaning isn't going to move you down the fast track any faster.

Luckily, one of the best by-products of your new college lifestyle is choice. And the single greatest skill you'll pick up here is the ability to use critical thinking in making sound choices.

******

Critical thinking works for me.

******

So let's apply some of that critical thinking to help you select a decent university. One way to make the decision is to let your parents or high school advisor choose for you. That can work and you won't be wasting any time you could've spent playing Halo. We'll sum this approach up as the "not making a choice is a choice of convenience I'll live to regret for the rest of my life" strategy.

If, on the other hand, you're into a little introspection, I can help you avoid waking up ten years from now with a "two point five kids, mortgage, two car, hate my job, hate my marriage, oh my god I'm my father!" hangover. To be honest, I can't guarantee that you won't become your father, Timmy, but if you do the following exercises you might end up a happier version of him, by going to a school that really suits *you*.

There are no right answers. All I'm asking of you is to think it through carefully and then evaluate how the choices you make now will affect everything in your entire future. Remember, it could be the difference between the good life and a life of destitution and degradation – no pressure.

Selecting The Right U 4 You.

Self Evaluation

Select the response that most accurately reflects the way you feel about each statement to help you select the appropriate type of college to attend.

Evaluation Statement #1

Money! The only valid reason for going to a school of higher education is to get a good job.

○ Yes, I especially like neckties, business attire, and sensible shoes.

○ College is the closest thing I got to free money and my dad threatened to make me get a job if I planned on living at home.

○ Whatever, did you see the hooters on that blonde just now?

Evaluation Statement #2

The knowledge I gain in college will provide me with inner strength, and will prepare me to face an uncertain world with clarity of forethought and earnest conviction.

○ Yes, this is me to a T.

○ Not sure, could you repeat the question?

○ Whatever, where's the party at?

Evaluation Statement #3

College is a place to bond with my peers. It is common ground for the elite in society to freely associate with one another… where future business, familial, and political connections are made.

○ Yes, Pa-Pa is a senator and I plan to be an investment banker.

○ Do these penny loafers look good? I feel like a dork.

○ Whatever, if you're not throwing elbows in the mosh pit we're cool.

Evaluation Statement #4

I plan on being famous and I'm using college as a launching pad where I can grow a fan base and practice my craft before going big time.

○ Yes, but I can't admit that in public without blowing my "street-cred."

○ I got some turntables at the pawnshop but I'm not sure how to plug them in yet.

○ Whatever, if you catch me at open mic Tuesday night I'll buy you a beer.

Evaluation Statement #5

I'm a big picture guy and I'd like to be a captain of industry. A degree will give me credibility. People will listen to me and do what I say because they'll assume I know what I'm talking about.

○ Yes, I want you in my office in five, and bring me coffee – black.

○ When you say, "...big picture" does that require photographic memory?

○ Whatever, you must be mistaking me for a complete dick.

Evaluation Statement #6

Prestige and pedigree are all important. Where I attend university is as important as what I choose to study. The name of the institution alone will open doors and raise eyebrows.

○ Yes, did I mention I'm going to be an investment banker?

○ If I get accepted, get a scholarship, and a really good tutor I should be set.

○ Whatever, as long as blazers aren't involved.

Evaluation Statement #7

Location, location, location... the physical environment of my school is what matters most. I like the: beach / mountains / city so much that if I wasn't close to it I'd die.

○ Yes, I'm a: surfer / snowboarder / climber / museum and pub-crawler and school is just an excuse I use to pursue my avocation.

○ I like Halo.

○ Whatever, have you seen the remote?

Evaluation Statement #8

A solid student exchange program is crucial. I plan on studying abroad so I'm more concerned with the ability to travel than choosing a specific degree path or American campus.

○ Yes, I love Europe, and Japan. After school I plan on cashing in on the developing economy of China.

○ When you look at the world map why is it that the *Middle* East is on the right side? – think about it.

○ Whatever, I'm still looking for the remote.

If you could choose to attend a different school, where would it be and why?

"I would choose to go to SMU, it's like the USC of the south, and God, southern chicks really do it for me."

– *Matt Countryman, Senior in Business Administration, USC*

What were your main reasons for choosing to attend the college you did?

"Cheaper was important to my dad, somewhat close to home but not close enough for my parents to visit frequently was important to me."

– *Kelly Miller, Senior in Communications, University of Arizona*

Acceptance Feels Good

Selecting a college that's right for you is only half of the challenge here, Sally. Suppose you make the call and your college of choice is all, "Oh, wow, yeah, I'm ahhh busy right now... ummm... you know, could you call me back some other time? It's like, not you, it's me... actually we're just not a very good fit... so... ummm... ba-bye, and have a nice life."

All of us will have to deal with rejection at one time or another but to avoid having to settle for a second choice, or skipping post-secondary education altogether pay attention to these details of the college application process and you'll at least know you gave yourself every chance to be "accepted."

It's Not You:
Throughout recorded history there have been numerous instances of the "It's not you; it's me" break-up line, and yet in every case it has always been "you" and not "me."

******

Entrance Exams

******

Outside of grades there are few criteria that will affect you getting love from the admissions office like your score on the SAT. Originally called the Scholastic Aptitude Test and then the Scholastic Assessment Test, it is now officially named just SAT. Even though the test makers themselves and the College Board, which hired them, agree that the test can favor males and whites, especially if they are affluent, the test has increased in use as a gauge for determining whether you are ready for an extended education. Like I've said before, this book isn't about "what should be" it's about "what is."

Yoda Voice:
There are many phrases within this book that sound very funny when spoken in the *Star Wars* character Yoda's voice.

Be The Test – You have been lucky enough to attend a high school that has a curriculum tailored to testing well on the SAT. You'll recognize that this is a trait of your school when you take the PSAT (preliminary) and all of the questions are verbatim to the ones you've just taken over the last four years. If that's the case for you, then when it's time to take the exam, you should be able to walk into the test after a wake-n-bake session in your buddy's '84 Ford Mustang around the corner from the school parking lot, and still feel confident that you'll do well. By the way, this is great preparation for how you'll take most exams in college. If you're not in a school like this ask your parents to move.

Be A "Rich Kid" – When your parents are alumni and can afford generous donations to the campus, especially if one of the buildings has your last name on it, your chances of getting into the school are pretty much a lock. If you show up for the SAT, spell your name correctly, and randomly check at least half of the boxes — that should be enough of an effort to show you're "trying." Use a number two pencil as instructed because otherwise you're just rubbing their nose in it.

Minor in Minority – Dealing with a university means you'll be hearing the words diversity and community a lot. They really do try to have a student population that reflects the society as a whole. So if you are a minority or come from a disadvantaged background you may receive some latitude in the review of your application during the admissions process, but an SAT score is a number that's hard to argue with – although organizations like FairTest.org will try.

VanWilderism #32
Why change your behavior
when you can just lower your
standards?
Write that down.

The thing is though, with the fight over affirmative action changing the rules daily, and the testing and alleged cultural bias not going away, the key to taking advantage of the system is to pass the test. My advice to you is… get help!

A student who has received coaching can expect higher test scores, but if you have trouble with the following sample test examples you may not only want to employ the services of the *Princeton Review* but you'll also want to think about getting *Margaret McManners Good Conduct School of Proper Behavior* involved too – just take a look and decide for yourself…

Van's SAT Preparation

Hypothetical Collegiate
Aptitude Examination Questionnaire

Question No. 1

Spatial Relations And Environmental Relevance

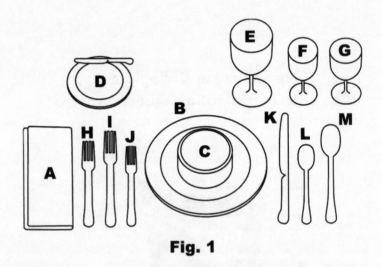

Fig. 1

According to Figure 1, which of the following items is *incorrectly* labeled?

○ I is a dinner fork
○ L is a teaspoon
○ H is a salad fork
○ E is a wine glass

Answers to Question No. 1

I is a dinner fork

Incorrect. The dinner fork, used to secure mighty slabs of roast for cutting, is the keystone of tined flatware. It is easily recognizable by its large size.

L is a teaspoon

Incorrect. While the necessity of a teaspoon at dinner, might at first seem dubious, given that coffee, brandy and cigars will probably be served to the diner after the meal in a separate drawing room. Its purpose becomes apparent when one considers: the teaspoon also functions as a dessertspoon. Without it, how can one possibly hope to eat the Crème Brulee?

H is a salad fork

Incorrect. Since the fork goes in the left hand, and as salad is always the first course to require a fork, the salad fork holds the outside left position as a matter of common sense. The fork has been correctly placed.

E is a wine glass

Correct. This is obviously a water glass. Only a first-term fraternity pledge with self-esteem issues and a severe drinking problem could possibly imagine that a glass of this size could serve as a fitting receptacle for wine.

Question No. 2

Language Arts – Object Association and Vocabulary

Which of the following conventions does not belong?

○ Rack of Lamb
○ Cabernet Sauvignon
○ Chardonnay
○ Merlot

Answers to Question No. 2

Rack of Lamb

Incorrect. Rack of Lamb goes well with Cabernet and Merlot, both red wines that should be served at room temperature.

Cabernet Sauvignon

Incorrect. Often called "the king of red wines," Cabernet Sauvignon is a dry varietal of red grape, grown mostly in France and Northern California, that complements rack of lamb nicely.

Chardonnay

Correct. Chardonnay is a white wine that is appropriately served with entries of chicken or fish and under no circumstances should it be served with rack of lamb. White wine is different from reds not only on the basis of color, but also because of the temperature at which it must be served – red wines at room temperature, white at a chilly 58 degrees.

Merlot

Incorrect. Second only to Cabernet Sauvignon, Merlot is often blended with the illustrious king of reds to produce a romantically full-bodied wine, the perfect accompaniment for an entrée of rack of lamb.

Question No. 3
Mathematics – Word Problems and Simple Calculations

On a par 3, a golfer's first shot lands in the bunker. He takes a practice stroke that hits the sand then proceeds to hole out three strokes later. What is his score of the hole?

Assume a modified Stableford scoring system is in effect.

- ○ Minus Two
- ○ Bogey
- ○ Minus One
- ○ Loss of Hole

Answers to Question No. 3

Minus Two

Correct. Though the player incurred a two-stroke penalty by grounding his club in a hazard, what would normally constitute a triple bogey, under the modified Stableford scoring system, the worst a player can score is minus two.

Bogey

Incorrect. Maybe at the municipal course where you play, but not according to the Rules of Golf available at bookstores everywhere. Consider picking up a copy.

Minus One

Incorrect. Remember that grounding your club in a hazard constitutes a two-stroke penalty. As Tom Watson often says, "learn the rules, and your enjoyment of the game will increase."

Loss of Hole

Incorrect. Do you even have a handicap? Although grounding one's club in a hazard does indeed constitute the loss of hole in match play, even the rankest duffer knows that the modified Stableford is a stroke play scoring system.

Question No. 4
Language Arts – Reading Comprehension and Critical Analaysis

A polo match lasts about one and one-half hours and is divided into six 7-minute periods or chukkers. Since a horse in fast polo can cover two and one-half to three miles per period, he'll be too tired to play a second one right away. After resting for two or three periods, some horses can return to the game. Still, in championship polo, a player will come to the field with at least six horses. The mounts are horses, mostly thoroughbreds, not ponies.

In a fast, but non-championship polo match, what are the fewest number of mounts that a player needs to play?

○ Four Ponies
○ Four Horses
○ Six Thoroughbreds
○ Twelve Thoroughbreds

Answers To Question No. 4

Four Ponies

Incorrect. Did you even read the passage??? Mounts are ALWAYS horses, never ponies. What kind of monster rides a pony? Somebody who kicks puppies, that's who. Are you a puppy-kicker???

Four Horses

Incorrect. Though a player could start a match with four horses, why would he? It not only makes the player look cruel to animals to ride them to the point of exhaustion, it makes the player look poor. Why not buy the additional horses? After all, it's only money.

Six Thoroughbreds

Correct. Due to the limited popularity of the sport, as soon as you enter a polo match, you automatically become one of the best players in the world. – Act accordingly.

Twelve Thoroughbreds

Incorrect. While the impulse to have a second string of horses available just in case a friend stops by is admirable, but is the telltale sign of the *nouveau riche*.

Remember, polo is a game played near stables, and stables sell horses. If a friend stops by, he will undoubtedly be able to afford to buy six top quality mounts of his own. After all, he's a friend of yours. And all your friends are loaded.

Van's SAT Preparation

Hypothetical Collegiate Aptitude Examination Questionnaire

Results:

You Got Zero Correct Answers

Raul, this is the fifth time you've taken the test and you still haven't gotten any correct answers? Please just quit now.

You Got One Correct Answer

Brush up on your rules of golf, and with a little luck you can hope to become a fine caddy. If you remember that your main job is to keep your eye on the ball and your mouth shut, you can expect a twenty-dollar gratuity at the end of the round. Not bad.

You Got Two Correct Answers

The life of a tradesman is good and honorable. Starting as an apprentice day laborer, you can expect to become bronzed and strong, and your skills will grow daily. Within ten years you can expect to be a foreman or on Workers' Compensation, both of which will constitute a nice stipend for your too-large family.

You Got Three Correct Answers

Not bad at all. You can look forward to a solid career in middle management. With twenty years of long, grinding hours you can expect to make vice-president and join a lesser country club. Only you'll be downsized and your pension fund raided. Your kids will resent you and your wife will cheat on you with the pool boy. But you will have given it the old college try, and isn't that what really matters?

You Got Four Correct Answers

Terrific. You can expect to get into the Ivy League school of your choice, and join an honorable profession, such as Medicine, Law or the Ministry, without sullying your hands in the sordid world of business.

Wow! With test administrators like this around here, you gotta wonder: who's running hell? – Am I right?

******

So to recap how to deal with the SAT so that it will help you get accepted into the school of your choice, do one of the following:

A. Coast thru the exam stoned because you went to a school that taught to the test.

B. Have wealthy parents (who am I kidding? If you're that wealthy you've already skipped ahead to the party school ranking).

C. Get a testing coach and/or be a minority.

What was your solution for staying up late and studying for an exam?
"My solution for studying all night is coffee and Aderol, legalized speed from the guy at the gas station next to the dorms."
– *Jessica Mills, Senior in Communications, University of Arizona*

An Essay
Is Worth A Thousand Words

Words are your friends, Timmy. String a few of them together and you'll have a sentence. Spend a long enough time on that path and pretty soon you'll have a story, or an article, or a top-notch essay that'd make us both proud. Did you know that my girl, Gwen used to write for the Coolidge College *Liberator*? She wrote some great articles: "Depression: Is Prozac really the answer?" "Famine: Crisis in Rwanda," and "Tracking Tuition: Where does our money really go?" Each article was well-written and researched, but those articles were skipped over by the majority of the student body. And I'll tell you why, Timmy. Because sex sells...

People want to read about hot bods and the battle over lite beer versus dark beer. They want scandal, the sports scores, and a few funny cartoons. In California I'm told they read their horoscopes too. What people don't want to read about is wasted tuition dollars, and famine, and depression, because... well, it's depressing. – *see Depression Is Depressing*.

You know who did read those articles? I did. I read those articles that Gwen wrote for the paper, Timmy. – Why? Because Gwen is a saucy hot blonde with a sassy behind? – Yes! But that's not the point... stay focused big guy. I read those articles because I love words. Words and the thoughts they convey. Without words we'd just be cavemen, or some sort of pet to an evolved species that did develop language skills. Maybe pet cavemen. – I don't know. What I do know is: I want to help you use a few words of your own as bricks... bricks and mortar in the foundation of two important documents that you'll need to tackle. – hmmm tackling bricks... Note to self: metaphorical mixology needs work.

******

The Personal Essay

******

During the application process you may be asked to write a personal essay. My suggestion to you Timmy is, "give the people what they want." Let's face it, you're life is boring. Spice it up with some stories of sexual innuendo, debauched behavior, and misdemeanors you may or may not have been involved in. Tales of ho's and forty ouncers...

Kidding. Just be yourself. You may not be Hemmingway or Tolstoy but tell them about something that makes *you* excited, and it'll carry the day. This isn't a resume, but if you've been lending a hand over at Habitat For Humanity or the local VFW, then this is a good place to let them know, but it's more important to express who you are, and why they'd be happy to have you around. Finally, keep it simple. Don't get too strung out on big vocabulary, and don't overuse the thesaurus either, because they're also looking for examples of good communication skills that meet the basic requirements of working at the college level.

John Latting: director of admissions at Johns Hopkins University says about the personal statement, "Be adventurous intellectually-write unconventionally. Applicants have more freedom than they think, and it's in their interest to use that flexibility." – *College Essays that Made a Difference*

******

The English Placement Exam

******

You will hear the following thoughts cross my lips but once Sally... be boring. Channel your inner dullard. – Hold on, I'm hyperventilating. Okay, I'm good. Thanks for being patient. When I was a freshman one of the hardest things I had to accomplish was getting into English 101. That's right, I placed out of my English exam at the sixth grade level twice. It wasn't until Ms. Haver, from the financial aid office saved me from myself, and got me "straightened out." I was having a "hard time." – Hey, this was long before our ...ummm "encounter." Look, I was in a bad place financially and we all make mistakes... don't ask, okay? PLEASE! – Don't ask.

She did keep me from starting my life at Coolidge in a remedial English program though. Seriously, it's a difficult test. How are you supposed to write without spell check or the paperclip dude? You'll never know how much you need someone until they're taken from you. Don't get me wrong, going back and polishing your written proficiency can be a good thing, especially if English is your second language, or if you're from Oakland (no offense, but Ebonics doesn't fly at the university level – I'm just saying...) – crazy professors and their silly rules of grammar.

Essentially Ms. Haver said, "Mr. Wilder, you are trying too hard to tell an entertaining story. Instead focus on something simple. Concentrate on good thesis structure: statement, body, conclusion, and use rudimentry – rudementary – rude... (sorry) rudimentary English so you'll make fewer mistakes." In other words, write at the ninth grade level and you'll place into a college level course.

Go figure.

Van's Personal / Placement Essay
Do's And Don'ts:

Personal Essay – ***Do*** tell a compelling story about **you**.

English Placement Exam – ***Don't*** make it complex.

Do stay away from Ms. Haver. She's stronger than she looks.

What was the one thing your parents said to you that really stuck with you?

They said, "Hey Robbie, we aren't going to pay your bills forever."
That really stuck with me, because I thought, "Well, then who the hell is going to pay them after that?"
– *Robbie Pickard, recent graduate, UC Irvine*

The Self-guided
Assessment Quiz
And Making
A Political Correction

You probably think of yourself as being pretty well adjusted, culturally and socially adept. And you probably are. Just by entering college you have set yourself apart from seventy-five percent of adults, and if you manage to finish your postsecondary education and get a bachelor's degree, you'll be a member of a select club, that equals just fifteen percent of the adult population of this great land. Timmy, stop to consider for a second that, beyond your classes, there will be intangible knowledge and experiences to be gained. That the select group of college grads you are aspiring to carries a responsibility to lead, to be exemplary citizens, and to apply not just the knowledge of course study, but what you've learned by these intangibles, to create a greater good for everyone. Oops, I'm starting to sound a little Chairman Mao-ish.

Seriously though, you're entering the culture of college. You are going to be challenged with new ideas of others and self. It's probable that you will grow from the experience. That is, of course, if you keep an open mind, and decide to jump into the pool of new experiences head first. Make sure it's the deep end – you don't want to break your neck.

Here's the deal. While you may find your uncle Bob's holocaust jokes to be fun, and using the N-bomb to be proper punctuation to end a sentence, or declarative statement, you'd be wrong. At least you'd be wrong to continue these practices in a larger society like, say, a university's diverse student culture. If you do, you'll likely end up with a broken nose and a disciplinary record. And besides, you'd miss out on a lot of fun that you'll only get when you participate in cultures that aren't your own. Because, let's be honest, no matter what culture we're talking about, there is one universal truth, Timmy. No one likes an A-hole.

Not only will you be exposed to new and exciting people and ideas, but you'll be afforded the opportunity to enhance these new experiences with mind altering substances that, when not applied properly, may hasten that broken nose and disciplinary report. Commit the following to memory: D.H.S.B.R.G.L., or:

Drunk

Homophobic

Sexist

Bigots (with an appetite for prescription pain killers)

Rarely

Get

Laid.

Oh sure, there are the exceptions, but unless you see yourself headed for a career as a Fox News personality, or becoming another Rush Limbaugh, I'd suggest you listen up.

There will be two offices on campus you'll hopefully only come into contact with occasionally. Depending on the campus you attend they may have different names, but the idea's the same. They are: the Office Of Diversity and the Campus Health Services Program.

These offices exist because your school is making an effort to keep you healthy, to give everyone space and a chance to, "just get along." It's likely that you'll be asked to take a self-guided quiz

Sensitivity Training:
During World War II, psychologists were used in group settings by the military to help soldiers deal with traumatic stress disorders, which lead to encounter groups and other methods that promote sensitivity to others.

dealing with one or more of the following: sex, alcohol and drug abuse, and racism and sexual orientation sensitivity. These quizzes are meant to provide students with a better awareness of potential problems, and resources to deal with them. They're also collecting data, Timmy. So don't screw around when you're taking these things. You don't want to end up in a lot of PC training courses, and the rest of us don't want to pay for well-meaning but expensive programs to straighten your drug addled racist butt out.

As a primer see how you fare on these self-guided quizzes...

******

Self-Guided Quiz No. 1
SEX

Check the box that most accurately reflects the way you would normally complete the sentence. Add the scores for each sample and compare your cumulative score against the recommendations provided. Note: complete the sentences as if you were the subject of the sentence regardless of sex, race, or cultural origin.

Male Masturbation:

A guy was caught jacking-off behind the sound equipment during marching band practice twice in one day. This is...

○ really nasty.   0 pts.

○ not a good place to hide.   5 pts.

○ me. 10 pts.

Female Masturbation:

A removable showerhead is a girl's best friend because...

○ cleanliness is next to godliness.   0 pts.

○ every angle deserves equal treatment.   5 pts.

○ just reading a Delta Faucet catalog makes
   my feet tingle.   10 pts.

Pornography:

An example of the way I feel about porn is…

○ even small PDA's make me hurl.   0 pts.

○ I watch Girls Gone Wild for the plot.   5 pts.

○ I have my own website – membership is
   just $9.99 a month.   10 pts.

Body Image:

When I stand naked in front of the mirror I think…

○ OMG turn out the lights.   0 pts.

○ not bad, but I wish I hadn't eaten both
   of those 14" pizzas last night.   5 pts.

○ holy crap, I'm stunning.   10 pts.

Pregnancy:

A girl is most likely to get pregnant from…

○ unprotected sexual intercourse.   0 pts.

○ a bf who uses condoms that are past
   their expiration date.   5 pts.

○ my finger.   10 pts.

Virginity:

I am still a virgin if…

○ I've never slept with anyone.   0 pts.

○ I've only slept with my bf / gf.   5 pts.

○ I've slept with everyone in my dorm,
   the baseball team, and all of my instructors,
   but I haven't told anyone yet.   10 pts.

Self-Guided Quiz No. 1
SEX

RESULTS AND RECOMMENDATIONS

Cumulative Score = 0 to 20

Most young adults that admit to becoming sexually active at an early age say that they regret not waiting longer. So you shouldn't feel pressured into doing anything you don't feel right about. You also probably have a good understanding of STDs and personal hygiene.

But in my experience, the ones who've broken out of a repressed or cloistered upbringing turn out to be the biggest freaks. Why do you think the most popular fantasy costumes are of private school girl uniforms, nurses, nuns, and policewomen? When the time is right you'll know it. Just be careful, you don't want to break any of the original equipment. It doesn't come with a warranty.

Cumulative Score = 21 to 40

Most colleges have good programs to help kids adjust to their new sexual surroundings. So whether you're active or working on dreadlocks for your palms, you should take advantage of the information and services they provide. There are also online forums, support groups, and courses you can audit that can provide an understanding of how other kids feel and act. Another option is to ask an older sibling, which might be entertaining, but probably not as informative.

Cumulative Score = 41 to 60

The infirmary is down the hall and to the right. Ask for Stu. – Don't thank me. Thank Penicillin.

Self-Guided Quiz No. 2
SUBSTANCE ABUSE

Check the box that most accurately reflects the way you would normally complete the sentence. Add the scores for each sample and compare your cumulative score against the recommendations provided. Note: complete the sentences as if you were the subject of the sentence regardless of sex, race, or cultural origin.

DON'T ABUSE YOUR DRUGS

Drinking Terminology:
The proper spelling of the term used for distilled or fermented spirits is...
- ○ Alcohol
- ○ Alchol
- ○ Beer

Drinking Apparatus:
Beer bongs are...
- ○ a dangerous way to drink because the user forcibly ingests an unusually large amount of alcohol in a very short period of time.
- ○ cool, just remember to hold your nose.
- ○ best used before breakfast.

Cannabis Sativus:
Smoking marijuana is...
- ○ an impediment to clear thinking and short term memory.
- ○ fun before: movies, a day at the beach, doing art, playing in my band, reading a novel, sex.
- ○ like breathing.

Methamphetamine:

Snorting crystal meth...

- ○ is for bikers, low-riders, and losers.
- ○ smells funny and makes my skin crawl.
- ○ kept me up for eight days straight, but I aced my mid-terms, fixed my stereo (twice), and my room has never been cleaner.

Binge Drinking:

Consuming large quantities of alcohol or binge drinking...

- ○ becomes a problem for a lot of kids in school.
- ○ is o.k. as long as you're in your dorm and by yourself.
- ○ is what I do on Thursdays.

Methylenedioxymethamphetamine (MDMA):

Taking ecstasy...

- ○ creates holes in your brain.
- ○ is fun when I'm out dancing, but I always drink a lot of water, and I forget how to pee.
- ○ makes me want to touch you, your girlfriends, and myself – hugs?

Self-Guided Quiz No. 2
SUBSTANCE ABUSE

RESULTS AND RECOMMENDATIONS

Cumulative Score = 0 to 20

You are sober and you plan on staying that way. That's to be commended. Two things though: if you change your mind somewhere along the way, get educated on what you're putting in your body before you put it in your body, and go slow. Your fellow partiers are years ahead of you in becoming a repository of toxic soup, and thus have tolerance levels that would make Robert Downey, Jr. blush. Don't become one of those sad and tragic stories that begin with, "It was her first time to try anything…"

Cumulative Score = 21 to 40

You may not believe this but I, Van Wilder, decided to go without alcohol for an entire year. I kept saying, "I can quit any time I want, I just don't want to right now." After a particularly rowdy New Year's Eve party that lasted well into February, a friend called me out, saying something to the effect of, "You quit? Yeah right! Hahahahahaha." So I decided to put my sobriety to the test.

I was successful for nine months until my birthday rolled around, which I figured was enough time to prove my point, and for my buddy to forget the bet. I felt good about myself. I lost a little weight, and I was a very cheap drunk for about two months. You know what the hardest thing to deal with was in those nine months free of drinkie drink? Figuring out how to turn people down for cocktails and still keep up socially. Everyone wants to have a reason why you won't do shots with them. "You gotta a drinking problem?" "You gotta a problem with me?" I found mentioning the bet was the best excuse. Besides being true, drunks can understand the appeal of gambling.

Cumulative Score = 41 to 60

A detox every six months, rehab every three years, and a complete blood transfusion every decade might keep you alive until you're forty-five. – Cheers.

Self-Guided Quiz No. 3
DIVERSITY

Check the box that most accurately reflects the way you would normally complete the sentence. Add the scores for each sample and compare your cumulative score against the recommendations provided. Note: Complete the sentences as if you were the subject of the sentence regardless of sex, race, or cultural origin.

Gay Lesbian Bi-Sexual and Transgender:
During the GLBT Day gay pride parade, the lead baton twirler kissed the head of the marching band. This...
○ was so beautiful it made me cry.
○ makes me horny.
○ is gay.

Race And College Sports:
Whenever the only white guy on the basketball team goes in the game...
○ I hardly notice he's playing because he's a forward and my favorite player is a point guard.
○ all of my friends stand up and cheer.
○ all of my friends stand up and cheer... Wig-Ga, Wig-Ga!

Race And Academic Standing:
All of the oriental students sit in the front of the class, skew the grading curve, and never share notes. I think...
○ that's o.k. Maybe other students should try harder to be friends with them so they'll come out of their shells a little.
○ "typical Asians."
○ I'll start a high-tech company and hire them at cut-rate wages to run it for me.

Male Homosexuality:

You're gay...

○ and that's nice for you.

○ because you wear sequins and glitter to class.

○ and I won't talk to you because I'm afraid you'll ask me out.

Female Homosexuality:

You're lesbian...

○ and that's nice for you.

○ because you wear the same black leather jacket and red ropers to class everyday.

○ can I watch?

Sexual Harassment:

A female student is trying to earn extra credit in a course that she's struggling in, by studying with the male TA. He suggests that there is an easier way to earn a decent grade, while he massages her inner thigh. This situation...

○ is a classic example of sexual harassment.

○ depends on whether or not she likes it.

○ is awesome! Where do I sign up to be a TA?

Self-Guided Quiz No. 3
DIVERSITY

RESULTS AND RECOMMENDATIONS

Cumulative Score = 0 to 20

You're probably well adjusted and you've had the good fortune to meet a lot of different people in your life. But please, spare everyone else the righteous indignation. Here's a thought: one sign with a clever slogan placed on the quad is enough. A thousand is overkill.

Cumulative Score = 21 to 40

Stereotypes exist for a reason. People will always tend to associate with other people that resemble themselves. When they do, they also tend to act like each other. Taking on the same characteristic traits, both good and bad. Guess what? It's true for you too sport, but if you make a point to party with a lot of different people and occasionally open your mind to the benefits of cultural richness you'll be a bigger person for it.

Cumulative Score = 41 to 60

Sensitivity training was invented because of people like you. – Thanks a bunch.

What's your attitude about skipping class and when do you decide that it's ok?

"Skipping class is totally justified when it involves drinking, shopping, or tanning."

– *Jessica Mills, Senior in Communications, University of Arizona*

How do you differentiate people in your mind, for example by race, sex, physical appearance, abilities, popularity etc?

Males: physical stature and/or alcohol consumption ability.

Females: Hot blondes… and everyone else.

– *John McCue, Senior in Neuroscience, UCLA*

FITTING IN

BRB 2 IM U
ABOUT E-COMMUNICATING

Put down the mouse, Sally, and step away from the keyboard for a second, and ask yourself these three simple FAQs. IRL as apposed to your virtual life do you...

A. end sentences with LOL for no reason?
B. go to sporting events, parties, concerts, or any other public gathering for the express purpose of collecting pics for your pages?
C. have a friend named Tom?

I thought so. Technology is supposed to make your life more efficient and less stressful, not more complex and time consuming. You're probably spending most of your time wondering if you should change the BG image on your MySpace page (because it's kind of lame now), IMing more than talking F2F, and tagging facebook pics of random people you only know peripherally.

******

U R living UR life vicariously through your gadgets.

******

Bong Logic From Hutch:
The problem with the youth of today? The Internet, dude – fries their brain cells.

Flog:
A fake blog.

You don't want to be a total PITA to yourself and everyone around you, do you? Deciding which IP or network you should post your blog to, or whether you have the time to keep up with more than one are not the most pressing issues in your life. I'm telling you, you've got to put a little distance between you and your virtual-self. So put the celli down when you're at the cash register. It's rude. You'll realize how true this is when you have to take a job in the service industry. Seriously, it's a wonder more people aren't strangled in that situation. Talk to people, not their toys, it's a mantra to live by.

Unless you're taking advantage of improved communication technology by really communicating something of value, then the whole enterprise is NFG. I understand that you might have a BF or BFF that you need to be in touch w/ 24-7, or that your LDR is requiring a lot of TXTing, but you're looking a little pale. – I hear a brisk walk and sunshine is a good cure for that.

You are faced with a choice: spend your time taking digital photogs and vidz, talking on the phone, TXTing / IMing / e-mailing, and updating your blog / MySpace / facebook pages, or you can have fun. You know that three-letter word that begins with an "f"? Calm down, Sally, I'm not suggesting to you that those things aren't fun, and I'm not suggesting you get rid of your PDA (in this case a Personal Digital Assistant, not a Public Display of Affection). OMG NFW would I recommend that! I'm one of the biggest gear junkies on the planet. Let me tell you w/o Bluetooth it'd take me most of this century just to synch my schedule and address book across my phone, notebook, desktop, etc., etc.

What I am saying is that, you know and I know, there are times when you are compelled to give out WTMI. OTTOMH – I'd guess that 90 percent of your e-mails, TXTs, and v-mails are a WOT, because you haven't thoroughly thought through what you want to say, and you haven't made a firm decision or plan, regarding the subject of UR MSG. FYI too much communicating without ever saying much becomes a lot of white noise.

Oh sure, Sally, you're probably ROTFL right now but I can save u a lot of time and aggravation when it comes to e-communicating. Besides being clear about what you're saying, don't delay a decision by putting it on future communication.

******

IOW if UR BF is out, and U R studying,
and U want 2 hook up L8R, say so.

******

Try saying, "Come over at ten. I should be done by then." Do not say, "Call me when you guys are headed over to the King's Head." Because when you do that, he'll call to tell you they aren't going over there after all, and they're headed to Joey's place. But you'll be in the kitchen when the phone rings, and you won't check your voicemail, and then you'll TXT him when it gets L8, and he won't get it, because he'll forget to turn the vibrate on, and Joey always plays the stereo super-loud, so he won't hear it either. You'll end up at the bar looking for him, and he'll be wondering why you haven't called back.

By the time you do actually talk, you'll both be :#) and PO'd, because you think that the other person has blown you off, and the only logical thing to do in that situation is to get snockered. You'll proceed to get into a ridiculous public argument while screaming into UR cell. You'll bring up bad hygiene, family lineage, and the desire to make each other entrees consisting primarily of feces. Not good.

OTOH it does leave you available when that QT from ECON 207 gives you a booty-call at 2:30 a.m. – LOL.

A Drop In The Photobucket:
Many sites affiliated with social networks are watching and collecting stats on you and your pics.

Acronyms
For The Acronym-oramus

YW	You're Welcome
WYSIWYG	What You See Is What You Get
YBS	You'll Be Sorry
YGBSM	You Gotta Be S**tin' Me!
WYSITWIRL	What You See Is TOTALLY WORTHLESS IN REAL LIFE!
WTMI	Way Too Much Information
WTF	What The F**k
WOT	Waste Of Time
WFM	Works For Me
WAG	Wild A** Guess
TXT	Sending Text Messages
Tlk2UL8R	Talk To You Later
TMI	Too Much Information
THX	Thanks
TIA	Thanks In Advance
TCOY	Take Care Of Yourself
SUP	What's Up
STFU	Shut The F**k Up
STFW	Search The F**king Web
RT	Real Time
RTFM	Read The F**king Manual (antiquated)
RPG	Role-Playing Games
ROTFL	Rolling On The Floor Laughing
ROTFLMAO	Rolling On The Floor Laughing My A** Off
ROTFLMAOWPIMP	Rolling On The Floor Laughing My A** Off While Peeing In My Pants
QT	Cutie
PU	Smelly
PO	Pissed Off

PITA	Pain In The A**
PDA	Public Display Of Affection
PEBCAK	Problem Exists Between Chair And Keyboard
PAW	Parents Are Watching
OTOH	On The Other Hand
OTTOMH	Off The Top Of My Head
OMG	Oh My God
NFG	No F**king Good
NFW	No F**king Way
NIFOC	Naked In Front Of Computer
N/P	No Problem
MTF	More To Follow
LY4E	Love You Forever
LTR	Long-Term Relationship
LTM	Laugh To Myself
LOL	Laughing Out Loud
LMAO	Laughing My A** Off
LDR	Long-Distance Relationship
L8R	Later
K	O.k.
KISS	Keep It Simple Stupid
KIT	Keep In Touch
JIC	Just In Case
JK	Just Kidding
JMO	Just My Opinion
IOW	In Other Words
IPN	I'm Posting Naked
IRL	In Real Life
ITIGBS	I Think I'm Going To Be Sick
IWALU	I Will Always Love You
IMing	Instant Messaging
IC	I See
GR8	Great

GMAB	Give Me A Break
GF	Girlfriend
GAL	Get A Life
GIGO	Garbage In, Garbage Out
FYI	For Your Information
FTBOMH	From The Bottom Of My Heart
FUBAR	F'd Up Beyond All Recognition
F2F	Face To Face
FAQ	Frequently Asked Question
eMSG	E-Mail Message
EOM	End Of Message
EOT	End Of Thread
DOM	Dirty Old Man
DIKU	Do I Know You?
CU	See You
BTW	By The Way
BRB	Be Right Back
BTA	But Then Again...
BFE	B*tt-F**k Egypt
BFF	Best Friends Forever
BF	Boyfriend
B4N	Bye For Now
ASAP	As Soon As Possible
404	I Don't Know

For more abbreviations and TXT-speak see Brock's advice, "Don't Know Much About English."

Once More With Emoticon

:-) ...... Basic Smiley

:-{ ...... Angry

>:-(.... Agitated

d:-) .... Smiley w/ Baseball Cap

q:-)   Smiley w/ Baseball Cap
         On Backwards

:-< ..... I'm Sad And Frowning

:#) ...... Drunk Smiley

o[-<]:. Skater

:-T ..... Keeping A Straight Face

:-x ...... Kisses

:-D ..... Laughing Out Loud

8:-) .... Cute Little Girl

~:-(.... Steamed Smiley

*<|:-) .. Santa Claus Smiley

:-> ..... Sarcastic

+-(..... Smiley Shot Between
        The Eyes

:-/ ...... Skeptical

;^) ...... Smirking Smiley

:-i ...... Smiley Smoking A Cig

B-) ..... Smiley Wearing Glasses

;-) ...... Winking variation

l-O ..... Yawning

:-(0) ... Yelling

:-(...... Sad Smiley

:~-(.... I'm A Cry-Baby

(:- ...... I'm Speechless

:-! .... I'm Bored

:-.) ..... Cindy Crawford

*<):o) .. Clown Smiley

:-@! .... Screaming Profanities

(:-| ..... Egghead

>:) ...... Evil Smiley

#:-) .... I'm Having A Bad Hair Day

:-# ...... My Lips Are Sealed

:8) ...... I'm A Pig

P-(..... Arrrgh A Pirate Smiley

:-t ...... I'm Sad And Pouting

=:-) .... Punk Rock Smiley

%-) .... Staring At The Screen For 12
        Hours Without A Break

(8-{)} .. Smiley Wearing Sunglasses,
        Mustache, Beard

:0 .... Surprised

':-) ..... I'm Sweating

:-0 ...... Talkative

:-[...... Vampire Smiley

[:-) ..... Smiley Wearing An iPod

$-) ..... Yuppie Smiley

What'er You Trying To Tell Me?
Assicons

(_!_) .... Ass

(__!__) .... Fat Ass

(!) .... Tight Ass

(_._) .... Flat Ass

(_) .... Half Ass

(_*_) .... Sore Ass Loser

(_#_) .... Taking An Ass Pounding

(_$_) .... Money Coming Out Your Ass

(_-$_) .... Cheap Ass

(Y) .... Butt

(_^^_) .... Bubble Butt

{_!_} .... Swishy Butt

(__)(__) .... A "WIDE LOAD" Ass

(_X X_) .... A Kicked Ass

(_x_) .... Kiss My Ass

(_X_) .... Leave My Ass Alone

(_zzz_) .... Tired Ass

(_o_) .... Ass That's Been Around

(_O_) .... Ass That's Been To Prison

(_?_) .... Dumb Ass

(_o^^o_) ...... Wise Ass

(_E=mc2_) .. Smart Ass

(_13_) .... Unlucky Ass

(_Lame_) ..... Lame ass

(_jack_) .... Jackass

[_!_] .... A Hard Ass(Mom)

(_) .... Tattooed Ass

(_%_) .... Average Ass

That's Titti-licious
Boobicons

(o)(o) .... Boobies

(O)(O) ...... Big Boobies

(*) (*) .... Perky Boobies

(,) (,) .... Droopy Boobies

\ . /\ . / .... Grandma's Boobies

(_)(_) .... Mamogram Boobies

(#)(#) .... Sore Boobies

(o)(q) .... Pierced Boobies

( )Y( ) .... Wonder Bra Boobies

(+)(+) .... Ready For Baby Boobies

($)($) .... Silicon Boobies

(^)(^) .... Cold Boobies

(@) (@) ..... Boobies With Big Nipples

[_] [_] .... Android Boobies

(p)(q) .... Tasseled Boobies

()() .... Boobies Against A Shower Door

\( )-( )/ .... Boobies In A Bikini

(o)(o) .... Bad Boob Job Part 1

(o)(o) .... Bad Boob Job Part 2

(o)(O) .... Bad Boob Job Part 3

SSN
Stands For Silly Screen Name

SuperWannaB • Ugly-spice • FinalbrdgPASS •

Nearlydave190571 • CzarOfHeaven • Ninjarid •

• ArrrgMeeEyePATCH •

• ScoobyObgynSnakz • KryptoBaBy47 • PEENISinaJAR •

• GuRLFacesitR • alanchikJunkie • Bj4agirl • Lovelyrockerbillion •

• YoGalightCub • puppyGiggles • Bill15g4y •

• Nuttinlikevengeance • chiquitaBear • PotentialMax •
• Freonmaster722 • javasurfer • PsychNeogreat •
• foreverCharmsU • effulgentJS810 • Evil8R • XoXoInFeRnO57 •
• SandRecipe115 • KamiKweefer • Monkeysynchrojin •
• LawnPiNkless • SpuffyDead469 • DramaKiller • bigglasting1 •
• borgLover • PhatlightPoet • vulturebot • stoopTheEvil666 •
• CoolChibi • Finalgood673 • ChoniRIDER • Jenni5eCr3trap •
• Bunnycent732 • GhoulLuv • bubblering84 • Spuffyfan012 •
• ScarletBeaver • ICEtasticular • AuthenticAbOvEX • Zeetherallxxx •

Drunk Posting Disease

Alert! There's a disease sweeping through the youth population. There is no known antidote, Timmy, no remedy for this dreadful scourge. Like many viruses it starts out as a simple organism and mutates into an epidemic, a pandemic, the plague... *ugh*. What once seemed harmless, something to giggle about, a passing fad, is now a crisis. No Timmy, I'm not talking about herpes. I'm talking about something far more embarrassing.

******

Drunk dialing is a gateway activity.

******

Drunk dialing is a gateway to drunk TXTing, which leads to drunk posting. I know you've gotten drunk dials before because Sally accidentally rang me a few times, thinking I was you. BTW she's got an impressive collection of lingerie. Sorry, I asked what she was wearing. It's a reflex. It's my privation, can't be helped. I'm just not able to resist asking, "What're you wearing?" when a pretty girl drunk dials me. We all have our crosses to bear. But dude seriously... meow.

You see that? Right there, Timmy, you're getting upset. You see what happens? Your girl has a shot or two, or a half dozen, misdials a digit or presses the wrong autodial, and the next thing you know she's telling one of your buds all about her crotchless pink teddy, with the red satin trim, and heart-shaped hole in the rear.

I'm telling you this because I like you and I want you to understand how awful this drunk posting affliction can be. Let's take this scenario a step further. I'm not trying to be the ghost of phone-sex future, but this is important stuff so hang in there. Here we go… It's late at night, Sally's at home, inebriated. She's tired of leaving messages on your voicemail (or your v-mail's full, same diff) and she's already left you two drunk TXTs. So she's surfing the net, waiting for the wonder bread, spaghetti sauce, cheese toast to get done in the toaster oven, and she clicks on your page. She makes a post. And then goes to her best friend's page and leaves a post about what she just wrote on your wall. Then she goes to Dane Cook's MySpace page – whoa girls sure do get wild and post some risqué stuff on his wall, she was tipsy and frisky, so don't ask what she put up, I can't take you there. She comes back to your page and leaves another post. She checks her page to see if anyone's responded to her. She starts randomly posting to friends of people who've tagged her. God forbid someone else is drunk posting too, because now it'll spiral completely out of control.

The cheese toast gets burnt to a black smoldering crisp. This is where things get scary… once she gets the smoke detector shut off, she is suddenly inspired to take pics of the molten, charred mess she's created. Who knows when the muse will strike? And once it does it'd be a crime not to share one's art, so posting the pics are the next logical step. Now, Timmy, don't be upset but think: your girl is lonely, trying to reach you, undoubtedly horny, and drunk. She's wearing panties and a tee, and a good portion of her midnight snack... and she has a camera and an Internet connection. You see where this headed don't you, Timmy?

******

Drunk posting can lead to public humiliation.

******

Now, what would've been a little silly late-night chitter-chat has become an embarrassment, maybe not of epic proportions, and I might've gone a bit overboard with that whole disease / virus analogy, but you get the point. As an example of how bad it can get, here are a few drunk posts that I've come across...

yeah! so glad i giot to see you tonight!!! im isss you zo mush

******

hey baby, why don tyou tell that boyfriend of yours to hit wish his best friend a happy birthday! huh, he forget where his roots lay? MJ never forgets abrothers bday....so not MJ
PS plaes shit on my face ASAP

******

come back and see me at lipsa kiln. now. i miss you and my holtzie. come for the weekend! Isia and i will get ya'll
DDDDDRRRRRRRRUUUUUUUUUUNNNNNNNNNNNNKKK
(as i am right now.)
love you!!!! miss you!!!!!!!!!!

******

Justo let u now, i would want to get back to gether w/ real bad. If we had ben going out n the frist place. Sow where deos thiss leavs us??? Balls with you.

******

K, ur an ass. I never see u anymore and u still have never slept with me :(... ANyway, have a great break! P.s. Call me sometime.

******

I deleted all my numbers when I was hammered

******

Hello pals. I was a little intoxicated and accidentally deleted all my numbers last night. I apologize for being lame and making a facebook group, but it's the best way to getting the numbers back. I love you all pls pls pls leave me a msg w/ ur numbers.

******

ijus want tell you .you are the best ting thas ever happen me bro. Thanks for taking me under your wint and teach ing me to be legit. womeday I'm show my children the pictuer I hav of you in my wallet. ha ha

******

hi:) Honestly all I need is closure... why her and not me? Am I not good enough for you?? I need you to tell me why, besides Cu. We're over... not on facebook I know... but we ar I need to know why you chose HER over me..... I gave you me feelings and I thought that was enough... why!!! Bye 4 no :(

******

what the hell why did u lower me down in your friendship level indicator?

******

dude did i even see u last night? i was like comatose 30 minutes after i got there. i remember meeting ur friend, then like waking up on my sisters front lawn. christ almighty, take a bite

******

hey sis just checkin in makin sure no one got u knocked up and to ask u when u comin home. love you

******

K, idunno why yours not witing me back but im getting anger. Key word "getting, (not there ye t) I thnx god everday that I joined the frat with you in it and my lif would MEANINGLESS you want make me better man... haha

******

Hey I ike ur new photo. is reminded me of a porno I watched the other day. REAL good 2 lol. We shuold chilll sometimes. oon!!!

– See what I mean?

Proper Professor E-mail Etiquette

I could fill the rest of the *Van Wilder Guide To Graduating College In Eight Years Or More* with proper online behavior, but then I'd have to change the name to *Van Wilder Guide To Not Being An E-tard*. So here's one last thing about e-communication to contemplate. Communicating with professors using e-mail should be viewed in the same way as talking to them in person. You are addressing a member of the faculty – a learned scholar. He or she is someone who holds sway over your future. And yes, you are paying their salary, but unlike conversations you've overheard your old man having with public servants, this is no time to let him or her know how you really feel. Don't forget it's also in writing, so there'll be no excuse if what you write is in poor taste, lacks clarity, or the proper decorum.

Besides being polite, be literate – as apposed to being illiterate (see drunk posting). Introduce yourself properly. Use your first name and last name. Identify the class you're in. Typically a professor will encounter thousands of students every year and if he's been around for a while then he may either be as bored, or as intoxicated, as you typically are, so the likelihood of him knowing you on a first name basis, especially with you showing up only on alternate Tuesdays, and sitting in the back corner of an eight-hundred student auditorium is very slim. I know this is a shock to you but not everyone in life is going to recognize you on a first name basis, just because you have their e-mail address.

Come to the point quickly and make it clear what you want to know. If you're asking a question about information in the class or lecture and it's going to be involved ask to get on his office schedule, or offer to come by if it's going to be difficult to answer your question in an e-mail. If you need to ask for a favor like taking a re-test, applying for extra credit, or contesting a grade, do it in

Myspace Numbers:
K-Fed = 73,104
Dane Cook = 1,781,954
Tila Tequila = 1,691,065
Satan = 17
– total number of friends as of January, 2007, Myspace.com

person. If it's to apologize for taking his daughter out on a date and leaving her stranded at a party, lie.

This is an example of how not to do it...

Subject:

Hey!

Message:

Hey professor! I was wondering if I could come into your office hours to talk to about my grade and taking the final exam. I sucked on this last exam but I was wondering if it is still possible for me to get an A. Thank you so much for your time.

Sincerely,

Matt

– Hmmm, not much to say that's not already self-evident, is there?

VanWilderism #11
If a cluttered desk indicates a cluttered mind, what does an empty desk indicate?
Write that down.

How many friends do you have on Facebook/Myspace?

"I have 1,027 friends on Facebook, but I personally only know 700."
– *Lexi Roderick, Senior in Communications, Arizona State*

Are online social networks addictive?

"Hell yeah they are. I'd say Myspace is like crack, and Facebook is like weed. Finding people's information on Myspace takes a little more effort, kind of like trying to get a hold of some crack. Getting girl's information on Facebook, like weed, is readily available, so you use it more."
– *Robbie Pickard, recent graduate, University California Irvine*

Rivalries
And Other Childhood Stories

For argument's sake, Timmy, pretend that you have an identical twin brother. We'll call him, Tommy. Now imagine that the two of you are nine years old. You are sitting at the breakfast table eating cereal. It's a Saturday morning so you've slept in and you're full of energy and curiosity about your young little life – *ahhhh*. Suddenly you are consumed by a question: if you and your brother are identical and you like Lucky Charms, why does he like Fruit Loops? You pose this philosophical question to Tommy, "Why do you like groady Fruit Poops instead of delicious Lucky Charms?" You follow up this insightful inquiry by dumping a heaping spoonful of your cereal into his bowl.

One thing leads to another until you find yourselves seated in front of the living room TV set. You and Tommy keep tally of how many times a commercial advertising your favorite cereal comes on, awarding a point for each viewing. You're both convinced that whoever has the highest score will be the coolest and the household champion. The two of you are jumping up and down screaming and waving your arms every time a commercial break comes on, and sometimes for no reason at all. Picture it: you're dressed in your mom's green print flannel pajama pants, your dad's green safari vest, and a felt hat, from your sister's starring role in her sixth-grade presentation of *Peter Pan*. You've pulled out your finger paints and used them to cleverly craft hearts, moons, stars, and clovers on your face, chest, and arms. Meanwhile you're wondering where your brother, Tommy, could have found a toucan outfit.

Don't you see how childish rivalries can be? It's the same with college athletics and competition of all kinds like, rivalries between fraternities, and academic competitiveness between students. Competition is good, and I love my Coolidge College Chickadees as much as the next fan, but some people take things too far. Take you and your brother for example, cereal commercial cheerleading? – Come on. I've seen and been in many arguments over best Ghostbuster or Ninja Turtle, but corporate shills like Cap'n Crunch and Tony the Tiger were always just soulless commercial characters to me. You guys really need to get something more serious to get excited about.

Timmy, I can hear you now: "But I don't have a brother named Tommy." And that may be true, but what you should be worried about is, if this sort of behavior persists into adulthood, you may have to stage an intervention to keep your twin's obsession with dressing in furry costumes from becoming a full-blown fetish. I know you love your brother, but who wants to deal with that?

VanWilderism #9
Revenge is a dish best served sautéed with a side order of melted self-respect and a garnish of spite.
Write that down.

Was face painting a huge ingredient of showing your team spirit?
"I went to UC Irvine, so we didn't have a football team. You look kind of stupid if you have your face painted to have lunch."
– *Robbie Pickard, recent graduate, University California Irvine*

Money
Is The Root Of All Purchases

My friend Josh once explained that there's a big difference between value and worth. He said, "If you really want to know what things are worth you should work in your father's pawn shop." Josh should know because he works in his father's pawnshop. Unfortunately for Josh you can't buy a college education in a pawnshop – It's true, I've looked.

It's unfortunate for Josh that you can't buy a college education in your father's pawnshop because Josh wanted to earn a degree in computer graphics. One thing though... the school he decided to attend didn't have any computers – *eeeyouch*. So I guess we can assume between his pawnshop and college experiences, Josh is an expert when it comes to the difference between value and worth.

Don't get me wrong, Sally, working in your father's pawnshop isn't a bad life and Josh is doing really well for himself there, but I'm sure he will tell you that a good value in an education isn't worth much, if the school doesn't give you the knowledge, skills, connections, and experience you were expecting.

******

What's it worth?

******

A dollar is just paper. Like a lot of people say, "You can't eat it," and "You can't take it with you." That is, of course, unless you're on your way to Cabo and then you should consider exchanging it for pesos. To determine the worth of something I like to think of money as a symbolic representation of a physical object. You can do this with anything really: an iTunes download, a Big Mac, PBR (by the can). I learned this from Grandpa Wilder. He was a farm boy so he used baby chicks as a relative object, but you know what? Baby chicks grow up to be chickens and they lay eggs and become grilled sandwiches, so their worth is always changing. It gives me a headache like calculus and being graded on a bell curve. So I tend to use twenty-two inch long party glow sticks as my object of relative worth – for some reason I go through a lot of those things.

Confused? Let me give you an example. Let's say the cost of a keg of Blatz *Milwaukee's Favorite Premium Beer* is valued at $39.99 – excluding tap and tub deposit, and the cost of a twenty-two inch long party glow stick is 35 cents. Then the relative worth of a keg of Blatz Beer is roughly equal to 114 party glow sticks. Get it?

Using this formula we can equate the "worth" of various college educations. Here's a chart that puts it into perspective for you.

Van's College Education Worth Chart

Value includes average total annual cost of: tuition, fees, room and board, books and supplies, transportation, and other expenses for the 2006-2007 academic year.

GLOW STICK WAR!

College Type	Value	Worth
Two-year public college	$12,000	34,285 party glow sticks
Four-year public college (in-state)	$16,000	45,714 party glow sticks
Four-year public college (out of-state)	$26,000	74,286 party glow sticks
Private four-year college	$33,000	94,285 party glow sticks

Now taking into account that a twenty-two inch party glow stick (I prefer green) comes in a 50-piece box that measures two inches by four inches by twenty-four inches, and considering a common freight container could handle roughly eight thousand boxes, if you were planning on attending Princeton University next fall you'd need to schedule three tractor-trailers worth of twenty-two inch party glow sticks to pay for it. Wow! Three tractor-trailers filled with twenty-two inch party glow sticks! – You can go with another color if you're not into green, but anyway you stack 'em that's a lot of twenty-two inch party glow sticks.

This is why I didn't attend Princeton University. Well, that and my high school transcript.

******

The Breakdown

******

Have you ever had a job Timmy? Ever had to be responsible for your finances? Pay bills? Rent? – Probably not. Chances are you're going into this without much in the way of discipline or practical experience with budgeting or long term saving. Well, the rubber on your money management skills is about to meet your Bursar's office payment plan pavement. So you really ought to know if you're behind the wheel of a cash flow black on black Cadillac Escalade with fat tires and spinners, or a day-glow purple Geo Metro with a missing rear bumper and maypops all around.

Don't look at me. My budgeting skills mostly resemble my golf cart: looks good, lots of environmental style points, but not much under the hood. Come to think of it, it doesn't have a hood... right.

I'm lucky. I have a personal assistant, Taj Mahal Badalandabad, an exchange student from Banglapur, India. Taj is great. I really love the guy. He's got heart, and drive, saved my life twice (metaphorically anyway), and as it turns out he's a fine accountant. My best advice for any college student having trouble with funding is get a personal assistant with a strong accrual skill set and unwavering dedication. When I was totally tapped and thought I was going to have to let Taj go he told me, "A good soldier does not leave his commander just because he lies wounded, arms torn off at the sockets, intestines spilling out onto the mud, picked at by the birds." – Graphic, huh?

Taj also said, "Van, the first thing we need to look at when dealing with your budget is the big picture. And then we will work our way to a breakdown." When my dad showed up the day before and informed me that he'd stopped payment on my tuition check my breakdown was more of the nervous variety. But thanks to Taj I got things under control. Here's how Taj explains the breakdown of an average college student's big-ticket expenses, minus psychiatric care of course:

Taj's Big-Ticket Breakdown:
- Comprehensive Fee (tuition)
- Room (where you sleep most nights of the week)
- Board (that's food)
- Misc. (weed, bar tab, Frisbee golf green fees)
- Beer (beer)
- Books (you'll need these)
- Babes (they're fun but expensive)

Taj pointed out that there are many items on the "list o' stuff you have to pay for out of your own pocket now that your father has cut you off at the fiscal knee caps" that can be reduced or eliminated. Here's a partial list:

Other Expenses You Might Have Missed:
- Clothes (what birthdays and Christmas are for)
- Laundry (what trips home on the weekends are for)
- Hair Cuts (going punk or hippy will help but it might limit your circle of friends and pool of potential dates)

Tuition and fees (2005-2006):
  $32,097
Room and board (2005-2006):
  $9,578
Est. personal expenses (beer):
  $2,675
Being able to pronounce
"Havad" without the r's…:
  priceless.

- Parking Fees (I recommend faculty parking, but make sure you've made friends with the campus police first. Tearing up tickets, or insulting "rent-a-cops" are bad ideas – entertaining but costly)
- Health Insurance (ask mom)
- Online Poker Debts (ask your ISP to put a child protection lock on access to your favorite sites, or double down, whichever feels right to you)
- Pizza (there's no way to cut the cost of pizza, deal with it)

******

Your Parents Are Mentally Impaired

******

No offense Sally, but your mom and dad aren't likely to be giants of Wall Street finance. By the time you're ready to attend college they'd need to be David Blaine to escape the budgetary shackles, straightjacket, Plexiglas case filled with water... and sharks, death trap of a family financial crisis they've created. I think the bank calls it the "let's take a trip this summer, the house needs remodeling, I've always wanted a new car, we can take advantage of the housing boom with a third mortgage" college savings fund.

So where's the money going to come from if what you're budgeting for school is worth three tractor-trailers filled with twenty-two inch long, green party glow sticks, and what's in your college savings fund is a tired old blinky, and a tube of glow-in-the-dark lip gloss?

When I was in school the only A's I got were in Professor McDoogal's freshman economics class, and tennis. You know what I learned Sally? That I like short tennis skirts? – Yes! And I learned that if you want a healthy economy you gotta spread it around. Spend it to make it. So when you're feeling pinched don't sit at home on the couch clutching your change purse. Take the plunge. If you're never going to be able to afford an Ivy League education o.k., whatever, don't let that stop you from pursuing higher learning.

For me taking my last seventeen dollars to a strip club turned out to be the best investment I could've ever made. Taj, Hutch, and I went to catch Desiree, my favorite exotic dancer at the mid-day all you can eat lunch hour buffet and chili con carne blow-jobfest, at Bubbas 'n Babes Gentlemen's Club. Taj got his first blowjob! It's a little different from what you might expect. Desiree is a master of her gastronomical releases – basically she farts on the customers. Surprisingly Taj got very excited; apparently in Taj's country that's considered the ultimate aphrodisiac. – I did not know this.

Desiree is quite amazing. Not only was she a big attraction on center stage during the lunch hour buffet and blow-jobfest, but she was also a grad student and teacher's assistant at Coolidge. Suddenly, right there in the front row of Bubbas 'n Babes, staring down my last single as if it were the last piece of currency I'd ever hold, just as that greenback was blown from the stage by Desiree's discharge, an idea bloomed in the bowels of my mind. As the vision expanded and wafted up into my consciousness I knew I was on the verge of something great. In that moment Topless Tutors was born. It was an entrepreneurial enterprise of infamous success, but that's another story.

VanWilderism #208
If it's not worth duct taping, it's not worth keeping.
Write that down.

So while going to a strip club with your last seventeen dollars is not a perfect solution to all of your economic problems, or might not be right for you at all, just remember when you're struggling put the right energy out into the world. Try paying a bill. In my case I was paying one bill at a time.

Did you call your parents more often to just "talk," or rather because you were in desperate need of money?

"My mom usually always did the calling in order to "talk" so I relied on her to call. I never needed to call for more money because I had their credit card."
– *Stephanie Stearns, Senior in Nutritional Sciences, University of Arizona*

Scholarships
Are Like Free Money

I'm not messing around with this section. You want some aid? I'll give you some aid. – One word, Sally. FAFSA. Actually that's an acronym, but everyone treats it like SAT, MBA, or BFD. In actuality it is a BFD, Sally. Filling out and filing the Free Application For Student Aid is the first step on every student's financial aid journey, and sometimes the first step in a long journey is the hardest. In this case it depends on your parents. You recall that mentally impaired couple we talked about in the last section? You remember, the people who clothed you, feed you, and gave you a place to sleep, but somehow forgot to save enough for your tuition? – Yeah, those guys. They're the same people you are now going to guilt into doing their income tax returns by February second of every year, so you can file your FAFSA early.

******

FAFSA requires income tax information.

******

By doing this your application will be on file well before the deadline when everyone else's shows up late, and you won't have to guess at the correct information at the last minute. Even if you consider your family wealthy you'll be surprised at how little they actually earn. Now you know why they drink themselves to sleep every night.

O.k., so you have your FASA filled out, time to kickback and wait for the leprechauns to come sliding down their rainbow to deliver your pot 'o gold college trinkets, right? Wrong! Consider this: if you take a forty-hour workweek to do the research, fill out the forms, and write an essay to get 20,000 dollars worth of grants and scholarships, then you'll be making 500 dollars an hour. That's right, 500 dollars an hour.

Most federal grants are based on need and not merit. So apply for these if your family income qualifies. After that there are a lot of scholarships out there for the asking. You just have to find the right people to ask. Start with your university. Make sure that the financial aid office has all of your information and your whole story.

******

Computers are stupid machines.

******

If you have extenuating circumstances, like a parent has just been laid-off, or your house burned to the ground, let the school know. Make friends in the financial aid office. Make an appointment for the summer to go in and get advice. They're not as busy then and they'll remember you later, especially if you're polite and smile. Remember the person's name that you talk to. It always helps to remember names and smile. Watch out for Ms. Haver though. I've said it before, "she's stronger than she looks."

Do some extended research beyond the school, and get creative. Look for aid from alumni programs (especially if your

Over $122 billion: the amount of financial aid that was distributed to undergraduate and graduate students in academic year 2003 – 2004.

VanWilderism #4
Worrying is like a rocking chair.
It feels good, but it doesn't get
you anywhere.
Write that down.

parents attended the school), your church, your parent's employer (even if they don't work there anymore), and corporations with offices or plants in your hometown.

Don't stop looking for aid after freshman year. Actually, after you've completed a year or two is the time you should be ramping it up. Get listings of organizations (public and private) that support your field of study, and contact them to find out if they offer college assistance. Look for research grants to get involved with on campus and ask professors who have fellowships if they need help. Many times the prof can hire you directly or get you aid, or both.

You'll be amazed at how much money is available out there. College kids are lazy, so a lot of funds go without applicants. Here's a mantra, repeat after me: 500 dollars an hour... 500 dollars an hour... 500 dollars an... Great, keep it up.

If you ever did drugs, would you sell them for some extra cash?
"Hell yeah I would do it. How do you think I bought this jacket?"
– *Anonymous*

Student Loans Are Like Free Money With Compound Interest And Monthly Payments

The first and only thing to understand about student loans is: you have to pay that mess back! Let me introduce you to your future worst nightmare, compound interest. Here's how the program works. You ask for money from a lending institution, which is backed by the federal government's student loan program. You get the money, which goes to the school for tuition, and with a little extra budgetary planning you can get a new iPod thrown into the deal too. As long as you are enrolled as a full-time student, you won't have to make any payments. The following year, you ask for more money. The financial institution gives you more money. You give the money to your school. Repeat.

There are caps to the amount you can borrow from these programs each year, and there are caps on the total amount you can borrow for your entire college career as well. So if you plan on spending more than five years in school, which is when most of the federal programs cut you off, then you'll want to find alternate forms of income. I say, why worry about that until at least the fall semester of your second junior year?

Borrow • Educate • Good Job • Payback Loan

******

Well at least that's the way the program is supposed to work. Hopefully, you don't end up on the "borrow, spend, take-a-break / never-come-back, minimum wage, boomerang kid, basement dweller, payments 'til you die," treadmill. You're not going to go out like that though, because I believe that you will graduate, Timmy. It's like I told you the day I met you on that rooftop, "…you'll make it here at Coolidge because you've got the balls to go all the way." – Relax; I'm wearing pants now.

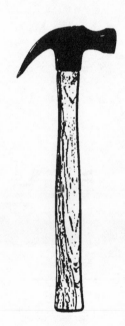

Before you go nuts with the student loan program, we gotta talk interest and payments. Your calculator probably has a compound interest button on it and there are several places on the web you can find calculation functions to help you. There are good ones specifically designed to help you calculate student loan debt at www.finaid.org, and www.collegeboard.com, but the calculation is always based on the following equation.

$$FV = PV\ (1 + i)^n$$

Where FV = future value, PV = present value, i = interest rate, and n = number of payment periods. This formula works for both investment and loans. In this case we're talking loan.

Are you asking, "So how much will I owe, and are you still wearing pants?" Very astute questions, the answers are, "Yes, thanks for asking and quite a bit." The average student in 2004 borrowed 24,000 dollars to get his degree. The average interest rate on student loans is about 6.8 percent. You might elect to pay that amount back over ten years with a monthly minimum payment of 50 dollars. On this schedule your monthly payment will be 280 dollars. The actual tab at the end of the payment schedule, when you add the interest to the principle of the original loan will be 33,000 dollars. So you've paid 9,000 dollars worth of interest to the bank in order to borrow 24,000.

You know this doesn't feel like enough cash to me. I think we should look at maxing everything out. Let's really blow the doors off this sucker! – Yes, my pants are still on, Timmy, pay attention.

There are two major lending programs, the Stafford Loan, and the Perkins Student Loan. They each have their own interest rate, payment schedule, and caps on yearly borrowing. To make it easy let's just look at the maximum amount you can borrow. The Stafford Loan will allow you to borrow 23,000 dollars over five years of undergraduate study, and the Perkins Student Loan will lend you 20,000 dollars over those same five years. Combining the two loans you can receive 43,000 dollars.

There are also PLUS loans that require mom and dad as co-signatories and are lent without federal backing so the rates vary and many universities don't participate, so ask. There are also second and third mortgages on the house, and regular consumer loans. These loans require whatever rationale you think will work on your parents to get them signing on the dotted line.

We'll concentrate for the moment on what *you'll* be on the hook for. Taking the same compound interest formula we'll find that the 43,000 that you borrowed, paid back over a ten-year period, will actually be worth an additional 16,000 dollars in interest and come to a total of 59,000 dollars. Sometimes I wish I had gotten a degree in banking instead of leisure studies.

"But Mr. Wilder, how do I get to stay in school for eight years when this money only takes me to five?" Damnit, Timmy. You're really stressing me out. It's hard enough doing computations without your whining too – *scheesh*. O.k. listen, I'm going to take my pants off. Whew, much better. Now I can think. I'm no expert at this, and Taj is off to grad school so he's no help, but here are a few suggestions that might work…

- Take out every loan you can at the maximum amount: Stafford, Perkins, PLUS, GATE, maybe throw in some merit or needs grants like PEL. Live modestly and spread the money out over time.
- Take your loan to Vegas each year in the week between receiving the check and when it's due at the Bursar's office. Hold back enough to stay drunk for the rest of the week in case you lose.
- Invest your loan money in a digital camera and a catchy web domain. This is the kind of thinking that launched Microsoft and Dell. – At least I think that's true, hmmm?
- Do like I did: "Spend now, worry later."

One or two last notes on loans before we move on: if you do only pay the minimum of 50 dollars a month after you leave college, your grandchildren will have to pick up the payments, and if you use the loans for anything but school you might be in violation of some state and federal ordinances. – Just saying.

Part Time Jobs
Are Painful

Here's a very simple premise, Timmy: you are going to college so that you DON'T have to work a menial job. There are only a few good reasons to take a part time job, and they all include at least one of the following:

- Backstage passes
- Free booze
- Hot chicks – preferably in bikinis

There are extenuating circumstances that can affect this rule, see *Cheating – Bro Deals In And Out Of Class.*

Internships
The Golden Elevator

No doubt you've heard of the "golden parachute." No? It's simple: a big boss, say my dad for example, acquires a company and appoints himself CEO. He then writes an employment contract that says, "If I ever get fired, I get to have an amazing retirement courtesy of the stock holders." It's a pretty cool thing. You'll learn the details when you go to Yale to get your MBA, but I digress. Internships! You should get one. I never had one but I hear they're very good.

I probably would have gotten one too but who has time? I was always slammed with lecturing at the freshman crisis group every other Monday, spearheading the Save the Swim Team Speedo Spectacular, and the Bloated Belly Beer Bash to Battle Bulimia. And then there was Sick Boy, not a week went by he didn't have an ailment: shingles, hepatitis, crabs – that was his fault. Did he ever get that goiter thing... taken... care... No?
– Too bad.

Anyway, you should look into getting one of those internship dillios. I'm told you'll be able to skip the entry-level positions after graduation. And even though I'm not speaking from experience here, I'd think that there are several skills that you'll learn or "learn about" depending on how you approach your new "boss." Remember, most people are bored to death with their daily jobs so milk them for the inside scoop. Here are the valuable skills every intern should walk away with:

- Asking for a raise
- Negotiating time off
- Navigating rush-hour traffic
- Cheating the time clock

* Bonus for taking an internship: office supplies!

There's actually more to internships than access to the supply closet. I know, hard to believe, right? What's another bonus? Basically it's a big "Timmy career laboratory experiment." You get to play dress-up in the occupation of your choosing to make sure it's a good fit. Again I'm guessing, not having done it myself, but I'll bet these might be some signs to watch out for, that would indicate a change in major is in order, if you spot them during your internship experience:

- You're drinking coffee by the gallon and not by the cup.
- Your boss appears to be 60 and you know for a fact he's not even 35 yet.
- You've avoided the "freshman fifteen" but you've gained ten pounds in the first two weeks in the office. – Step away from the morning doughnut and bagel tray.
- Brain itch.
- Time spent in the restroom exceeds time spent at your desk.

My advice, learn the professional lingo, find out where the execs have country club memberships, ditch early, and make sure to get on the Christmas party guest list.

One thing about internships though, there aren't any internship elves dolling them out with little internship gift-wrapping and internship greeting cards. No, you gotta do some legwork on this one yourself, Timmy. Ask that friend you made in

VanWilderism #14
There is no "I" in "fabulous."
Write that down.

the financial aid office for help. Your school may also have a career guidance service, or your scholastic councilor maybe able to help too. So get on it.

About paying for school... How much money a week do you get from your parents? How much do you think you should get?

"My parents didn't give me any money, but they paid all my parking tickets, which probably came out to $200/month."

Is your student loan something that is "real" to you, or is it more out of sight out of mind?

"It was out of sight out of mind until I started getting the repayment bills in the mail last month."

How do you deal with it mentally?

"I dealt with the thought of paying my debt by drinking."

If you were to start paying off your loan now, how much would you start paying per month and how long do you think it would take to pay it off?

"Right now I'm at $200 per month for about 35 years."

Would you say you spend more money on food or alcohol? How much would you say you spend on each?

"Haaa...hahahahahaha. I would hate to spend more than $8 on a meal but somehow I had no problem dropping over $100 a night at the bar..."

– Jon Mccue, Senior in Neuroscience, UCLA

Student Jobs And Work-Study

Sally, I already explained this! Dude, seriously, are you sleeping again? Don't pretend to be taking notes, I can tell your eyes are closed. I'm not going to say this again. You are going to college to avoid menial labor. Resorting to a student job or work-study is at best plan C, after maxing out loans, grants, and begging on street corners. Work-study means you get to sell crap to the other kids on campus, or clean up crap that other kids on campus throw out, or clean up other kids' crap, after you sell them the crap that they just threw on the floor. If you were the A/V guy in high school and you get a job in the computer lab, maybe it'll work out but it's not likely.

I rarely look down on anyone, and God knows I love Coolidge, and I would do anything for the kids that keep it going, but gosh Sally, it's rough out there. All right, I can agree that not getting fired for sleeping on the job is a major plus for you. You've got me there.

VanWilderism #56
The best things in life are free, but there's a lot of very cool stuff that's extremely expensive too, so get a job.
Write that down.

Wealthy Parents
Are Worth Having

I have a hard time relating to not having enough money. Well… for anything really. I grew up with wealthy parents so I'm a little unclear on the whole poverty thing. On the other hand, having parents who have forgotten I exist, literally they forgot I existed, this I understand. – But money? No, I got that one down pat.

VanWilderism #213
The minute you settle for less than you deserve ask for a refund.
Write that down.

Suppose you aren't getting that extra grant money because your parents' income disqualifies you, or they suddenly cut you off mid-semester. I ask, "What kind of monster would do that?" It is awful behavior, but it happens. This is what I suggest you do at the earliest sign of trouble…

******

Divorce Your Parents

******

BEING THERE

The System...
A Bureaucracy Is Born

It doesn't take a rocket scientist to see that the university system is a bureaucracy. My friend Jay is a rocket scientist and he pointed this out to me (I don't know what that means, but it's interesting). The word bureaucracy is derived from the French, bureau, meaning desk, or later an office where desks are. The French language was always pretty confusing to me, but it's sexy, don't you think? Here's the thing, Sally, the word really took hold just before the French Revolution of 1789. You recall from your high school history that's the one where everyone lost their heads. We're talking guillotine city – *ouch*.

This French guy, Baron de Grimm, really wasn't happy with the way things were being run and in 1765 he said this about bureaucracy, "...indeed the public interest appears to have been established so that offices might exist." I take this to mean: sometimes jobs exist not because of the function they're charged with doing, but because of the work they've created to define their *raison d'être*. Ooh la-la. Could someone man the fire extinguisher, I'm smokin' tonight.

Whatever, enough with the French, I need to calm down, and they're a bunch of head loppers anyway, and that fella Grimm – really lives up to his name doesn't he? I understand dealing with any big organization can be a drag, but a bureaucracy is not

necessarily a bad thing. They exist because they function. At least at some level they do. They provide structure. It's important to know where stuff is and who's in charge of it. If it was anarchy maybe the librarian could be in charge of booking concerts or the building supervisor could run things over at admissions. Sure it would be fun, for about a day.

Plus it's handy to have a hierarchy in place to track the cash, and know who to ask to fix things when they go wrong. The way I see things, you have three options when it comes to relating to the college bureaucracy: despise it, ignore it, or make it work for you. Likewise, there are three avenues to making the system work to your advantage.

One: The student government and campus organizations like the Greek Council represent the interests of the general student body. You'll get to interact with wonderful power hungry, political, Skull and Bones wannabes like Richard Bagg, who was the president of the Coolidge College Student Government and head of Delta Iota Kappa. I mean, when I met him I could see he had DIK written all over him.

Two: Activism is empowering. Get involved. Raise your voice. It makes a difference. Why else would repressive regimes throughout history focus their destructive energies on crushing student speech? Oops, we're back to that head rolling business again... moving on.

Three: You can join clubs, fundraisers, and national organizations. Whether you're into Bare Bottom Bungee Jumping or the Save The Spandex Internet Disk Jockey Club, you'll find your niche.

Basically, by being a big bureaucracy the university ends up providing a component of the organization that you can get involved in. Thus giving you an opportunity to impact the dynamics of what's going on around you.

******

Your College Is A Corporation

******

Did you know that the Harvard Corporation is the oldest corporation in the western hemisphere? Yeah, strange to think of a venerated institution like Harvard as an ivory monolith of business and profit isn't it? In fact, it was incorporated by the Great And General Court of Massachusetts in 1650, which was a corporate colony at the time, which in turn was owned and operated by the Massachusetts Bay Company. So Harvard College was a corporation incorporated by a corporation. – Sounds to me like someone got a little corporation crazy.

As if you didn't know already, the corporate structure is based on the concept that a number of people purchase stock in a business, thereby owning a small portion of the company. In return for their investment they expect the business will turn a profit, which makes the price of their shares rise, and at times they receive a dividend, or portion of the income.

With the advent of mutual funds and other institutional investment pools, and the growing base of investors in the market, the individual becomes removed from the administration of the business, and frequently becomes focused only on the bottom line. So if you're the guy sitting in the CEO's seat you better make sure you're bringing in the green, quarter in and quarter out. – That's a lot of pressure, man. Guess what? It's not always healthy for the future of the business either, or in this case, the private college.

So, Sally, if you're wondering how this affects you, the public university student, then prop your eyelids open for a sec. – I've got a heads-up for you. For the last half-century America has experienced a dramatic growth in the college student population.

Tuition Bulge:
From 1981 to 2000, average tuition (adjusted for inflation) more than doubled at most post-secondary institutions while the median family income only grew at 27% during that same time. *finaid.com*

According to the US Department of Education, in 1940 sixteen percent of our citizens attended college, by 2001 sixty-two percent of high school grads went on to university.

So there are more students now, a lot more, which means more buildings, library books, professors, parking spaces, and more grass seed for hackey-sack areas. It also means more tuition money. But your tuition doesn't pay for everything. You get help from the "public," that means the government. You know, "we the people." The catch is, ever since the Reagan era of the eighties, college funding at the federal and state levels have been in steady decline. – Did anything good come out of the eighties? ...Big hair, day-glow, Duran Duran, ummm no.

By 2000 just half of a public university's annual budget was covered by the "public." – And after 9/11? Ohhhh, Sally, security doesn't grow on trees you know. So, yeah it's way worse now. More students wanting to learn, less money from the government to teach them with... what is a poor university president to do? Well, to start with, he'll begin acting more like a CEO and viewing the school as a business.

The public knowledge trust is now defined by: revenue streams, cost analysis, market research, and consumer habits. That's you Sally. You are a degree-hungry, career-path-seeking, college education consumer.

As the university inc. ship bobs on the fickle fiscal sea, the school has to look for other ways to offset costs. This comes in the form of corporate sponsorship from outside companies, elevating rock-star professors who land new patents and big grants, from both government and industrial sources, and expanding the administration of the university to include lobbying and marketing departments to bring in more "consumers" and "donors."

If that's what it does to the school, what's it doing to you? I'll tell you what it does... Your courses and degree programs are

State of Reduction:
Between 1985 and 1995 states reduced direct appropriations to universities by 25%
US Dept. of Education

being designed by and are increasingly being integrated with external corporate interests. The infrastructure of the campus, things like the bookstore and eateries, are being outsourced. Sometimes whole segments of the curricula, like distance learning, are being pressed into becoming self-supporting. You also get to pay more. – Nice.

******

You Are Not Powerless

******

As a consumer, your dollars are the voice of your desires. Student surveys do affect the planning of the university's board, so be wise with your responses. Also, by being closer to corporate donors and creating programs that reflect business interests, the curriculum and professors become more reflective of the real world. So I'm not saying that the college-corporate marriage is bad or good, it just "is."

I wonder… how many branding opportunities are there in one day?

VanWilderism #44
Live and let live. Be and let be. Kiss and be kissed. Hang out and be… wait, what?
Don't write that down it still needs some work.

Do you feel like an individual within the system, or just another student being "groomed" to fit the desires of society?
"I do feel like I'm being groomed to fit the desires of society… But after all I do love being pampered."
– *Alana Waters, Senior in Accounting, University of Arizona*

I Am A Powerful
Demographic

Yo, those throwback Adidas look great with your G-Star jeans, Busted Tee, and D&G leather jacket. Timmy, I hate to admit it but you are what you buy. And because you are what you buy, you are a powerful demographic. You're sexy, soon to be wealthy, and smart. You are the eighteen-to-twenty-four college demographic. In fact you're half of that demo because it divides along gender. Sorry to say, females at your age are more mature. They reflect on long-range purchases like homes, healthcare, and retirement investments, whereas you, Timmy, are more of a... how can I put it? – You're a knucklehead. Your moments of monetary contemplation are more repetitive and simple-minded. When you think at all about what and how to buy, your thoughts tend to run in the direction of: domestic beer, cars, imported beers, and porn. Both genders do have common habits though. They are consumed with consuming gadgets. *See BRB 2 IM U.*

There is probably no more pressing issue for companies producing consumer products, entertainment, or services than how to market their product to you. Think about it. What's the most important thing a company in today's advanced marketplace has to face? You guessed it, Brand Identity. They want, no... they *need* for you to identify with their product. When you sneeze are you reaching for a bath tissue? Hell no. It's Kleenex® or it's a snot-rag, are you feeling me?

In the long run, brand loyalty is everything. Consider how crucial it is for Brand-X to have you hooked on what it is they're selling. College grads have more discretionary income. They lead busy lives and fill those busy lives with lots and lots of stuff. Timmy, it's not so much what you buy now, but what you can afford to buy in the future, over and over again.

Plus you're one of the cool kids. You're the people everyone else is looking to, to set trends. Sure there's hip-hop and skate culture, but if you're not buying, more than likely, it's not flying. Not to stroke your ego any more than I already have, but when you graduate college you become part of society's success story. So when you've been marketed to properly, when you "buy in," you are the capitalist system functioning at its highest level, because what you buy at 1:00 on Monday, everyone else is lining up for at 3:00 on Thursday.

VanWilderism #2
Are you stalking me? Because that would be super.
Write that down.

Don't believe me? Break it down for yourself... Bud Lite or Miller Lite? Do you really give a rat's poo-crack? You may personally feel the need to fight to the death to defend your favorite, but when you look at the "eighteen-to-twenty-four college" demographic as a whole the answer is, No, you don't. But what if... what if, Timmy, to prove just how powerful a consumer demographic you are, every college student purchased only one of these brews for the next six months?

Word.

Do you feel at this age you tend to be very brand loyal?
"No. I'm not brand loyal because I'm in college... I just buy the cheapest stuff."
– *Greg Haber, Senior in Journalism, University of Arizona*

Are You A Commodity
Or An Individual?

Doctor, lawyer, beggar-man, thief… Does a job description by any other title smell as sweet? This is a big moment. It's pivotal. I'm pounding the table here… pound, pound, pound, bam, bam – ow. I've hurt myself. Ouuuu, hope I didn't break the skin. Whatever, I'm sucking it up, because this is a defining moment in your life. This is go time, the big Kahuna of monumental events. You are going to have to face this question sooner or later, Sally, so it's better you deal with it now.

******

Are you a product?

******

Up-pup-pup… Not so fast. Ask yourself, are you becoming what you think other people want you to be? – Your professors, your counselors, your prospective employer? Are you consumed with being packaged properly? Are the prerequisite line items filled out on your resume yet?

It's true, people make snap judgments and stereotypes do exist. People don't take the time, or never really have it to begin with, to evaluate the character and worth of every person that they interact with. They're practically forced to judge the book by its cover. When you're meeting someone for the first time in a business relationship, or you're in that first big interview, the way you present yourself will directly affect the way you're perceived, and it's very likely that it will determine the outcome of the business at hand.

******

You have one chance to make a good first impression.

******

Let me tell you a story. A buddy of mine, Glenn, was an engineering student, and he had this internship with an engineering firm that did a lot of business with military contractors. Part of his job was to go out to an air base and collect field data on some sort of gizmo or thing-a-ma-what's-it. – Very technical business that engineering. So he goes out there on his first day and has a really hard time with security. He was turned away before he could get any of the information he needed, and went back empty handed. The problem? Glenn was a punk rocker.

******

Security never trusts punk rockers.

******

The next day, same base, same basic security-check, Glenn skates through no problem. The difference being, he showed up this time sans multiple piercings, heavy rings, leather jack boots, and black everything. Instead he was wearing khaki pants, short sleeved white button down oxford, and mid-rise standard construction boots. He'd also noticed that all the regular construction workers on the base wore orange hardhats, and the supervisors all wore white ones and carried clipboards. So to complete the package he made sure to paste down his spikes and tuck them under his white hardhat, and to stop by the local drugstore for a clipboard. Not only was he allowed access anywhere he needed to go, he even got a couple friendly salutes.

The moral is that presentation is critical, but is that really who you are? Sure it was funny at the time, actually it still is a bit humorous, but Glenn didn't stop being a punk rocker. He stopped being an engineer, lives out in Hollywood somewhere I'm told. So, Sally, how do you define yourself? – Pre-law, pre-med, engineer, Avril Lavigne-hating mosh pit freaker? What makes you, you? What's in here? I'm pointing at *my* chest, Timmy.

Dude, you're a great guy and I love you like a brother, but I hope you're taking notes, so you can review them later, because sometimes I look in your eyes and all I see is… nobody's home right now please leave a message… beeeeeep. Okay, maybe that's a little harsh, sorry Timmy. I'm backing up like five paces. Wait I'm outside. Ding-dong, hello it's me your conscience. Hello…

******

You are your soul.

******

Whatever it is in life that gets your rocks off, that's who you are. Do it in exclusion of all else and you will be successful, or at least you'll be happy knowing you do what you love and what makes you feel whole. – Simple, right?

After graduation how do you wish to portray yourself to others, i.e. as an individual or as your degree or job?
After I graduate I want to portray myself to others as a Victoria's Secret model.
– *Alana Waters, Senior in Accounting, University of Arizona*

Majors And Minors

Timmy, Sally, sit down for a minute. Take a deep breath. Hold it. Hold it. Hold it. Exhale... Look at me. Look... At... Me... Right here, focus in on these words... Six months after you graduate you will be working in a field that has nothing to do with your major. – Shocked? If it happens, and there's a good chance it will happen, you will look back on this moment and laugh your buns off.

It's no minor incident deciding wisely what your major will be, but don't get too hung up on it. That's why I just walked you through the whole, *Am I A Commodity Or An Individual*, question. Ponder this...

- You can switch majors. In eight years there will be plenty of opportunity.
- Don't be shy. Ask professors about their discipline.
- Try a career in the field on for size. See *Internships The Golden Elevator*.
- Go with your natural abilities.
- Study something you love.

It's like that day during my final senior year. I attended my classes, just about stayed the whole time too, even went to a few that weren't mine. Stepped into the wrong one. Liked what I heard, stayed. – And the bonus, a notebook full of doodles. It's amazing what you can accomplish when you have an open mind.

VanWilderism #67
Ginger Rogers did everything Fred Astaire did, but she did it backwards, and in high heels. Which is pretty hot when you think about it.
Write that down.

You And Your GPA

GRADES
KNOWLEDGE

My father is obsessed with work. His whole life revolves around it, and I have never once heard him getting bummed out over bad marks in business. You see Sally, your *Grade Point Average* is one of life's many arbitrary yardsticks that you'll be judged by, and that you'll use to judge yourself, but I suggest you question its value.

******

A GPA is like a new car.

******

When you drive a new car off the lot the value drops substantially. It's a big drag but the upside is... you have a new car! In many ways a GPA is similar. Five minutes into your first job no one will ever ask you again about your GPA. Likewise, if you've taken my advice about internships, and working in your field, you'll be so far ahead of the employment curve that you will have passed the "so how were your grades?" threshold long before then. My point being, that beyond keeping your grades above failing...

******

Your GPA is meaningless.

******

I'm not saying slacking is the preferred way to go through your college life, not at all, I'm saying, be true to why you came to school in the first place, to get an education. Face it, 90 percent of what you learned even last week is already gone. It's ironic that most college towns have a bar across the street or around the corner from the campus library, which acts as an encouragement for to you build up your brain cells one minute, and to mercilessly kill them off the next. It's like they're creating an army of Einstein-Rambos. Learning how to study: where to find the information you're looking for efficiently, a realization of how you function mentally, and how to pull the right answer out of a sea of data is the deeper value here.

Grades are important in that they help you understand when you've hit the course's dartboard bull's-eye, and when you've accidentally impaled an innocent bystander in the shoulder. – I never promised no one would get hurt. You should go over your graded work once it comes back to you, so you can learn from your mistakes, and especially to help reinforce what you got right.

At the end of the day, Sally, your studies are all about balance. You'll find that you need some "easy A's" to help you juggle the demands on your time, but that many times the more difficult courses are the ones you'll walk away from saying, "That was totally worth it." You may find yourself challenged with the consequences of subverting your own beliefs in order to satisfy a teacher's point of view, or you might find a new perspective on reality when you realize there are commonalities between calculus, computer code, and an R&B classic's three-cord progression. My roommate, Hutch, explained that last bit to me. He was high at the time but I'm going with it anyway.

Average Is Good:
"And to you 'C' students, you too can be president of the United States."
– *George W. Bush during 2001 Yale commencement speech*

To help you keep your GPA at the University's required level here are a few tips to practice...

- Network with your classmates to find the best instructors and classes to take.
- Figure out *how* you learn.
- Work the system: ask for extra credit, contest grades (but never question a professor's grading habits in front of other students).
- Pretend to be interested in the course material. You might end up convincing yourself that it is worthwhile, and it's less likely to piss off the instructor.
- Balance your workload so you can apply yourself to the harder classes.
- Don't blow off an easy class. You'll need the 4.0 to balance the other 1.2's you're getting.
- Watch the average in a class where the professor is grading on a curve. That 50 you got on the mid-term might be worth a solid B at the end of the semester.
- Find out which classmates seem smarter than you, and then find out why.

Sally, the "real world" doesn't start after graduation. The "real world" is happening right now. We are the sum of our experiences and the knowledge we gain from those experiences. – Score another one for Hutch and his bong. So I ask you, what's more important, gaining knowledge or getting a good grade? Your GPA is a yardstick. It's a measuring tool, and like all tools, it's how you use it that counts.

In the "real world" you're judged by what you know and how well you apply it. Dressing well and smelling good helps too.

How important was your GPA to you?
"My GPA was really important to me, maybe because I want to continue my education either in graduate school or medical school. However, as I get farther into school, it is just not that important to me as it use to be. You know what, as long as you don't go below a 2.0 and don't get kicked out of school, whatever."
– *Anonymous*

Depression
Is
Depressing

I know it's hard for some people to believe, but even I occasionally get depressed. Everyone goes through low points. It's a part of living. It's impossible to be "on" all the time. Personally, I believe it's a good thing to get blue every now and again. You should embrace your moodiness, because if that's the way you're feeling at the time, then it's good to express it. When you keep it locked down inside it becomes...

******

A Big Bottle Of Repressed Depression

******

I say wallow in it, Sally. You've seen me there. I was somewhat smashed in my room and singing that song you thought was "so dope" (your words not mine). What was it called again? Oh yeah, "Gwen used me for her newspaper story, then married an asswipe and ran over my heart with a metaphorical truck," originally performed by Air Supply. It went something like: *I'm all out of love. I'm so lost without you... la la la.*

Yup, that's the one.

******

Depression isn't shameful.

******

Depression is not a sign of weakness. It's the opposite. You have to be brave to admit that you've got problems and to reach out for help. That business with Gwen was pretty hard on me but I got through it. I tend to get worried when it's day two, or fifteen, and I still can't get off the couch. You know it's time to bring in the pros when your head is full of "oughts-thay of uicide-say or umping-jay off the oof-ray like immy-Tay." I hear that just talking about your problems helps. Yes, I do agree that whomever you confide in, should under most circumstances, be wearing trousers. God, will I ever live that down?

Between school, work, relationships, money, and family problems, everyone you know is understandably stressed-out big time. So how can you tell if you or someone you're close to is clinically depressed? Well, singing songs by Air Supply indicates you're pretty far down that road, but according to the American Society For Suicide Prevention the early warning signs are…

- Binge eating or forgetting food needs to actually reach your mouth to be consumed.
- Trouble concentrating
- Constantly feeling tired
- Moving or acting in slow-mo
- Fidgeting
- Never sleeping or sleeping too much

Looking over this list reminds me of… every college student I've ever met. So if you're worried maybe you could just ask, "Hey, is everything cool? 'cause you look like crap." and then gauge their reaction. Try to resist the urge to say things like, "You have so much to live for." or "Think about how it will hurt your family." or "That's probably gonna leave a nasty stain."

Instead, try saying stuff like, "Things must really be awful for you to be feeling that way." Let the person know that if it's really bad you'll help them find a good therapist or counselor and that you'll go with them if they want you to.

If you are unable to get assistance or you think that it's crisis time, call 911 or 1-800-SUICIDE for help. Here are some signs that it's gotten out of hand...

- Loss of interest in usual activities
- Feelings of worthlessness
- They're headed to the bathroom with a bottle of Jack Daniels and a loaded revolver

Being depressed is nothing to be ashamed of, and it is serious. Find someone to talk to; a professional if necessary, and there's always medication – ahhh psychotropics. Ritalin... it's not just for breakfast anymore. Lastly, never underestimate the revitalizing properties of pity sex. I've done some field research, and I can conclusively say it works for me.

Reaper Bias:
There are more than four male suicides for every female suicide, but twice as many females as males attempt suicide.

VanWilderism #7
All you really need to be happy is scented candles, massage oil, and a little Barry White.
Write that down.

How did depression affect you?
"My depression made me transfer back to a school closer to home, but after a year there, I knew I belonged where I started my college days. So I transferred back. And I joined a sorority and it was the best decision I ever made. I have had the best time."
– *Anonymous*

Cheaters ~~Never~~ Prosper

We've covered who you are, what you're going to study, how important your grades are going to be, and how you'll get depressed by it all. Now the only logical response to get you out of that depressive funk is cheating. Recent history is littered with examples of successful cheaters: Kobe, Rose, Bonds, Palmeiro, McGwire, Canseco... Wait, I'm only thinking of sports stars, and they're not overwhelmingly successful as cheaters. I know I had a better example, some sort of presidential figure, but I've lost it. Anywho, when it comes to cheating we can just put down baseball players as a whole, with their stolen bases, stolen signals, and steroids as a league unto themselves. Kenneth Lay... cheated, lost, died, and got away with it anyway. According to the *Inquirer* every famous actor and actress alive today... cheated. And the clergy, can you say, "pedophile?" or maybe "male prostitute?" How about, "misappropriation of funds?" Yuck. Religious leaders, entertainers, civil servants, and captains of industry all have their share of cheaters.

******

You Are Conditioned To Cheat.

******

Timmy, it's clichéd, but when you cheat, you're cheating yourself. You've paid for an education, and the best way to make sure you get it is to do the work yourself. Outsourcing your research paper to an essay service in India may help a struggling third world nation get ahead in the global economy, but who's the real winner and loser in that scenario? – Come to think of it, this is an outstanding research paper for Business 310 -*Ethical Practices In Business Management*, which begs the question, "Is it research or cheating to outsource the work on that paper too?"

What is cheating anyway? Getting a bud to sign you into a class that you're paying for but blowing off? Sharing notes (or buying them)? Double-teaming an individual homework assignment? Cut-n-pasting articles or supporting arguments from Wiki? What if you post your work to the web and other people pick up on it?

******

Cheating = Getting Caught.

******

As I've pointed out, a college is nothing if not a bureaucracy and as such it protects its image at all costs. There are stringent rules articulated and there are punishments prescribed for cheating so as to achieve the illusion of propriety. I say illusion because… They don't want to catch cheaters because it ultimately ruins the image of the institution to have cheating scandals. I'd say that most students are mostly honest most of the time. However, for reasons like managing workload, offsetting extraneous requirements in classes outside your major, and happy hour most students mostly only cheat on occasion.

Not withstanding some students' belief to the contrary, professors don't like catching cheaters. When an instructor catches someone taking liberties with the honor code it renders their academic equilibrium unbalanced. They teach, you learn, the proof of your learning is in the test results or the paper you hand in, and when that cycle breaks down, they feel foolish and… cheated.

The university doesn't want to catch you because it looks bad, and the professor doesn't want to catch you because it feels bad, and you don't want to get caught because that would be stupid. Which brings me to my next point… getting caught cheating requires stupidity.

The Internet, friend or foe: Now that we all have the Internet it becomes very easy to slack off when it comes to composing that last minute paper. The problem is we *all* have the Internet. If you can spend five minutes using Google to search for an essay or blog entry to lift, then how hard do you think it is to track those same words back to their original source after you've turned them in as your own? To make matters worse, anyone who has attended a school that subscribes to turnitin.com will tell you the odds are against you when you jack phrases or entire sections of text from electronic sources. Learn to paraphrase, site your sources, and use the "clear formatting" function – no one wants to read text in five different font styles and broken HTML fragments.

To further avoid suspicion do as Alex Halavais, former director of the masters program in informatics at the University at Buffalo suggests in his blog entry, *How To Cheat Good.* "No. 6 – Use the word rediculous: This almost magical word will cause any instructor to instantaneously turn off all internal plagiarism detection." I have to agree, using the word rediculous, sounds so rediculous, that it would be rediculous to expect to find it in a published essay. By the way the proper spelling is r.i.d.i.c.u.l.o.u.s. Alex's seven other tips to keep you from getting caught cheating are pretty awesome too. – Google that sh*t, I did.

Bro Deals: One of the advantages to joining a fraternity is that you get a catalog of term papers, tests, quizzes, homework assignments, and exams that change surprisingly little from one semester to the next. So if you have Professor—X for course—Y and he's been teaching from the same material and syllabus for decades you are in luck, because your frat dues not only bought you new friends but they also earned you a peek at most of the course materials he'll be using.

Bro Deal:
A transaction based on the barter system, made between friends or close associates.

There are other ways to get that kind of information as well. As a party liaison I had many opportunities to trade favors for grades — No, Ms. Haver was not involved… this time. A prime example of favor trading being: A pass on the cover charge in exchange for tomorrow's quiz questions from a "friend" in the 10 o'clock class of my 3 o'clock accounting class – harmless, right? You can see how it works, Timmy. Everyone's got something to trade.

******

Your Future = Professional Cheater

******

We've gone through the gray area of cheating and now it's time to address the substantially grayer areas of cheating, as Winston Churchill once said, "When you're going through hell, keep going." I'm not 100 percent sure how that applies here, Timmy, but it always cracks me up, so I quote it a lot. Anyway, we can mostly agree most students don't cheat most of the time, but some students are on their way to becoming most professional at it. Step back from the whole ethical, moral, social, academic arguments about cheating for a moment, and accept that it is a part of our culture to cheat. We've also established that getting caught is stupid. So if I remember my Philosophy 110 logical statement diagramming correctly…

If *A* and *B*, then *C*

Where:

A = Some students cheat.

And B = Getting caught cheating is stupid.

Then C = A student who cheats well is not stupid.

Additionally, D = Stupid students who get caught were probably too lazy or not smart enough for college anyway.

– I audited Philosophy 110, so I might be paraphrasing, but this looks right to me.

What conclusions can we draw here, Timmy? Let's see, in order to be an efficient student you need to know when to cut corners, which requires networking, market force analysis, and financial deal-making skills. Then there is being capable of bending the rules, and rationalizing it to yourself and to your accomplices in order to continue your questionable practices. You'll also need to be able to evaluate the resources at your disposal and when you can afford to outsource. Sounds a lot like almost every CEO and corporate exec my dad hangs out with.

My friend, Gerard, who is from Texas, at one time had the distinction of being the only professional jazz drummer in Dallas. When I asked his brother, the chiropractor, how professional jazz drumming was working out for Gerard, he said, "If you're not getting paid it's a f#@king hobby!" Wow. Gerard's brother sure knows how to bruise a buzz, but I'll tell you something, Timmy, he was right. The big idea here is, if you're going to be a habitual cheater, be smart about it and go pro.

******

Deny The Lie

******

A subset of cheating is lying. You'll need the ability to lie convincingly on those rare occasions that the system works against you or you get careless and get caught. The best lies work on half-truths and their success relies on their recipient's inherent desire to be lied to. Remember the professor doesn't want to catch you and the university doesn't want you caught. This is no time to be timid. Try using one of these declarations or some variation of them (by now you should be good at paraphrasing)...

"Of course that entry on Wikipedia has the same phrasing and the exact wording as those three areas of my thesis, I'm a member in good standing and I regularly update their database with my research."

"This? On the inside of my sleeve? Oh, that's my grocery list. I've designed a system that helps me memorize by substitution. It's a combination cross-reference study aide, and I get my shopping done too. I totally forgot I was wearing that today."

"Of course I'm familiar with easyessay.com. I write for them."

When you run into a situation where the aforementioned aren't adequate for your acquittal you can throw a Hail Mary with the following:

"If all of this generation's ethical role models consist of: politicians who cheat election results, corporate management that cheats the average share holder, religious leaders who cheat on their vows, prominent entertainers cheating on their spouses, and professional athletes who cheat their performances, then isn't my cheating on your test an indictment of the society in its entirety? And if that's true aren't you actually claiming that the United States of America is to blame? Well, if that's the case then the terrorists have already won!" At this point you should leave the room indignantly, but be graceful, you don't want to be a sore winner.

If you get away with that one, and succeed in diverting blame, then you should switch to pre-law. No question you'd make a great attorney.

VanWilderism #26
If you're not a winner, cheat. If you lose anyway at least look good doing it.
Write that down

THE VAN WILDER FILES

Panos Patakos
&
The Van Wilder Files

My three years at Coolidge College flew by so quickly, almost as fast as my run at MIT where I worked on designs for extra-planetary robotic probes. Science is a fascinating field, but not much in the way of popularity. No parties, no women, no fun. Most of all…no women.

Yes, it is a sad fact that a great GPA alone will not get you laid. Life is so unfair. As president of the Lambda Omega Omega fraternity, which regularly posted a 4.15 collective GPA, I recognized that we needed help. So when Van agreed to aid us in throwing a party… a party we could be proud of… a party people would actually show up to, I could not have been more overjoyed. The event was amazing.

Seriously, Van was a godsend. I would have paid him way more than a grand for that party. How do you put a price on dignity? How do you put a price on poonani? Thanks to Van, we meet our pleasure quota every semester, and then some! I discovered that there are women out there who enjoy men with a larger than normal medulla oblongata, and that Newton was wrong. A body at rest actually tends *not* to stay at rest, so long as my tongue is properly applied.

That party changed all of our lives. So when Van asked me to help compile the Van Wilder files, as a scrapbook of his time at Coolidge, I was more than happy to help.

COOLIDGE COLLEGE
Application for Admission
1995

PERSONAL DATA

Legal name:	Gender:
Wilder, Van	Male

Prefer to be called: (Nickname)

Just "Van" is fine

Permanent home address:

12 Randolph St., Darien, CT. 06821

Birthdate:	Citizenship:
December 13, 1977 - I'm a Sagittarius, with all that implies. I'm fiery, outgoing and more than a little sassy.	US

Possible areas of academic concentration:

Tantric Studies, World Music, Mixology.

Or there's always Economics. I can't decide.

Languages spoken:

English, Love

Possible Career plans:

Casino greeter; Own a beach, swim; President, US or Mexico.

EDUCATIONAL DATA

High School you now attend:

Winthrop Academy, Concord, MA 01742

Is your school public?	Private?	Parochial?
Good God no!	yes	

Date of secondary graduation:	College Counselor's Name:
June 5, 1995	Tom Hagen

List all other secondary schools including summer schools you have attended:

Vergerieux Falconry Academy

Venezia Academia dell'arte epee

The Learning Annex - Seminars include:

Reiki Healing Energy Massage, Boudoir Photography,

and Tom Vu's "Life too short to get rich slow" Real Estate Weekend

TEST INFORMATION

SAT: Verbal: Math:
            800   710

FAMILY INFORMATION

Mother's full name: Janice Wilder	Father's full name: Van Wilder
Is she living? Yes	Is he living? His personal assistant assures me he is. Oh, and he keeps sending me clippings from the <u>Wall Street Journal</u> about young entrepreneurs.
Occupation: Chairwoman of the council for the preservation of the performance arts	Occupation: I'm not sure exactly what it is that my father does, but it seems a lot like whatever Richard Gere's job was in <u>Pretty Woman</u>. Suffice it to say, that when it comes to the lucre, my dad's got gobs of the stuff.
College: Madeira	College: Coolidge
Degree: AA	Degree: BA
Postgraduate:	Postgraduate: Coolidge
Degree:	Degree: MBA

Please check if parents are   Married☐   Separated☐   Divorced☐   Other ☒
Let's just say there's a distinct chill in the air and leave it at that.

Give name and ages of your brothers or sisters.
    One Brother - Stanley, 12

    One Sister - Nancy, 15

ACADEMIC HONORS

Briefly describe any scholastic distinctions or honors you have won
beginning with ninth grade:

> The Farnsworth Diorama Prize - Given annually to the Freshman who
> makes the most compelling presentation of the First Thanksgiving

> The Brewster Ceramics Cup - Given for excellence in kiln-fired
> pottery arts

> The Phineas Trimble Forensics Award - 1992-5

EXTRACURRICULAR PERSONAL AND VOLUNTEER ACTIVITIES

Please list your primary extracurricular, community and family activities and hobbies.

> Varsity Basketball - motivational consultant

> Prom King 1992-5

> Saved the Marianas Nematode from certain destruction.
> Now it's merely on a protected list

> Wish Upon a Star Astronomy and Matchmaking Social Club, Chairman

> Committee to Establish One Nation Under A Groove

> President, "Rekindling the Flame." Reading Erotic Stories to the Elderly

> Detardation - Comprehensive Social Skills seminar for Dungeon Masters

WORK EXPERIENCE

List any job (including summer employment) you have held in the past three years.

> Sommelier - Le Fier Navet

> Condiment shopper - George Soros

> Echidna Wrangler - Ayers Rock Studio

> Photographer's Assistant - Snap-On tools calendar

In the space provided below or on a separate sheet if necessary, please describe which of these activities (extracurricular and personal activities or work experience) has had the most meaning for you, and why.

Whenever I undertake an activity, I like to throw myself 100% into the project. That means no matter what I do, from wrangling echidnas for the Australian horror film, "Spiny Death," to listening to the patter of summer rain on a wooden roof, the experience changes me profoundly. So I find it impossible to label just one extracurricular activity as "most meaningful."

But I would like to point out my extensive contributions to organizations that I believe make our world a better place. Last year I founded the "Wish Upon A Star Astronomy and Matchmaking Social Club." This group taught me what a special place a secluded planetarium can be to a group of hormone-addled teenagers.

I also served as chairman for the "Save the Marianas Nematode Society." Not only did we help get the world's largest deep-sea tubeworm off of the endangered list, but we also learned the value of water safety at our numerous Jacuzzi fundraisers. Two members of our group also set a new world record for the longest underwater kiss, even though it led to their suspension from the football team.

Speaking of damp underwear, I learned a lot about teamwork during my tenure as president of the "Rekindling the Flame" Senior Citizen Reading Group. I never would have imagined that it took at least four able-bodied teenagers to restrain an octogenarian school marm hopped up on herbal tea and a few too many chapters of Equinox. Thank God for Chlorpromazine.

In addition to my experience in peer clubs, I've also had plenty of experience working in what you adults call the "real world." I spent a summer working as a sommelier at the world-famous Le Fier Navet in downtown Manhattan. There, I learned the difference between the heady nose of Tuscan Chianti and the refined splendor of supple, medium-bodied Graves Rouge.

Last summer I worked for a friend of my father. I spent three months traveling as the personal condiment coordinator for investment guru George Soros. Together, we scoured the globe searching for rare ketchups, mustards and relishes. The best of which, by the way, are found in the city of Ihuru in the Maldive Islands.

This summer I plan to let my creative juices flow a bit. I've been selected for an internship as a photographer's assistant for the Snap-on Tool Calendar shoot on the island of St. Thomas in the Virgin Islands. Although the position is unpaid, I'm sure there'll be plenty to learn from the dozen bikini models on the trip. Can you say, "no tan lines." Yummy!

In closing, I'd like to thank you for your time and consideration. I hope that you find the experiences that I've related helpful when making your final decision as to my future at Coolidge College. Please be sure to send me your email address. I'd like to send you some of the photos from my internship in order to keep you abreast of my progress over the summer.

PERSONAL STATEMENT

The personal statement helps us become acquainted with you in ways different from courses, grades, test scores and other objective data. It will demonstrate your ability to organize thoughts and express yourself. We are looking for an essay that will help us know you better as a person and a student. Please write an essay (250-500) words on one of the options listed below. Please indicate your choice by checking the appropriate box.

☒ Evaluate a significant experience, achievement, risk you have taken, or ethical dilemma you have faced and its impact on you.

☐ Discuss some issue of personal, local, national or international concern and its importance to you.

☐ Indicate a person who has had a significant influence on you and describe that influence.

☐ Topic of your choice.

Stryker froze to death in front of my eyes. I had warned him about the dangers. But he wouldn't listen to me. Of course, he wouldn't have been Stryker if he had. Stryker was a cop, you see, and not just a beat cop. He was part of an elite riot-control brigade. I'm not sure what the exact acronym salad combination applied to his employer. Was he DEA, FBI, ATF? He never told me. I didn't press. He didn't have to tell me he was the best. I had seen him fight before, down in the subway system.

Some maniac with a rocket launcher and an electric net was rampaging through the city's light rail system, when Stryker caught up with him, armed only with a baton. I thought I was going to watch him die then and there, but I couldn't have been more mistaken. A dizzying series of punches and kicks culminated in a brutal uppercut that sent the deranged assassin flying onto the tracks. Just as the killer got up, still wobbly from Stryker's savage beating, a downtown express train came charging through the station and dragged him to a bloody death.

But Stryker was completely unprepared for his next opponent, the poor, cocky magnificent bastard. Within seconds, it was clear Stryker was outmatched. I wanted to help... Oh I wanted to. But there was nothing I could do. This combat was between two warriors. Though it be to the death, who was I to bring dishonor on my friend?

I watched in horror as the blue-clad assassin known as "Sub-Zero" covered Stryker in some kind of deadly liquid nitrogen brew and froze him solid. One swift punch, and Stryker shattered to pieces on the ground, an obvious fatality. For a moment, I could do nothing. Paralyzed by fear and horror, I wept kneeling in front of the icy fragments that had been my friend. They glittered like diamonds of the purest blue.

It was then that I realized in life we all face choices. We can submit to the emperor Shao Khan, living in fear of his shadow priests and Outworld extermination squads, groveling at the dark altar of his sinister sorcerer Shang Tsung, and hoping against hope that he won't feed on our souls.

Or we can train at the Temple of the Order of Light to be Earth's chosen champions in Mortal Kombat! We can follow in the blessed path of Lord Rayden and Liu Kang, offering our bodies as perfect sacrifice for the good of the world. I chose the latter path, and that has made all the difference. I also rescued the Princess when I played Super Mario Brothers, but that was pretty easy.

ALL APPLICANTS MUST SIGN BELOW.

My signature below indicates that all information in my application is complete, factually correct, and honestly presented.

Signature	Date
Van Wil	March 15, 1995

Booster Club Presents Senior With New Wheels

— *Courtesy, The Coolidge College Liberator*

Coolidge senior and philanthropist Van Wilder received a personalized golf cart at Sunday's ribbon cutting and dedication ceremony for the Trevor P. Wooten Driving Range. The Golf Team Booster Club presented the cart to Wilder as a token of its appreciation for his help in raising the money to rehabilitate the school's dilapidated practice facility. Last month, Wilder coordinated the club's Charity Drunk Driving Competition.

Over 100 competitors drank beer and hit the driving range in an attempt to earn enough points to win the coveted title of Greatest Drunk Driver on Campus. Each competitor's longest drive was measured out in feet, and was then multiplied by the number of beers consumed during their twenty-minute heat. The product of these two numbers determined the competitor's final score. Coolidge junior Bartholomew "Blowhole" Baxter won the competition with 2,696 points after downing eight brews and driving the small ball a whopping 337 yards.

The event raised over $20,000 for the club, well over the $7,000 needed to repair the driving range and putting green. The club board of trustees decided to use a chunk of the extra cash to thank Wilder with his very own golf cart. GTBC President Brent Whitman said that his club couldn't have accomplished its goals without Wilder's help.

"We owe it all to Van. He came in and made it all happen for us," Whitman said. "We made twice the money we needed for the improvements. The party was awesome, I got wasted. Van Rules!" When asked how it felt to have hosted such a successful event Wilder said, "I just wanted to do my part and to give back to the community. It feels good to help when you can." It was reported that Wilder is already planning the club's next fundraiser, The Co-ed Shirts vs. Skins Miniature Golf Tournament.

Van Wilder has been a "student" at Coolidge College for the past seven years, majoring in Leisure Studies. His advice column for the *Coolidge College Liberator* appears bi-weekly. Email questions to Van@coolidge.lib.edu.

ASK VAN

Who put the bop in the bop-shoo-bop-shoo-bop? And for that matter who put the ram in the Ramma-lamma ding-dong?
— *Vince*

Great question, Vinny. With 1,093 patents to his credit, it should come as no surprise to anyone, that it was the "Wizard of Menlo Park" himself, Thomas Alva Edison, who indeed first placed the bop among the bop-shoo-bop-shoo-bop. What may surprise you, however, is that it was Edison's long time rival, Marty Forshpan, who may deserve credit for the ram in the Ramma-lamma ding-dong.

In his autobiography, entitled *Thomas Edison Was a Stupid Lying Scumbag Who Stole All My Good Ideas,* Forshpan claims he had been working on the ramma-lamma formula for some time, and was foolish enough to reveal the secret to Edison at a drunken office Christmas party while the pair were discussing inventing something to make paper copies of their ass. According to Forshpan, Edison patented the idea the very next day, along with the carbon button microphone. And the rest, as they say, is history.

******

Did you kick my dog?

— *Carley from next door*

Let me respond to your question with a question. Did your dog deserve to be kicked? Let's think... Did Mr. McWoofles bark constantly? Did he hump legs? Did he bite all passersby? Was he, in fact, a Presa Canario in a Yorkshire Terrier's clothing? As I recall, the answer to all these questions is a resounding "yes." Yet, as dog lovers such as myself know, no breed of dog is bad by nature. Only their owners can make them that way. So why blame others, Carley? You want to know who kicked your dog? You did!

P.S. If Mr. McWoofles tries to squirt his vanilla love-pistol on my knee one more time, don't be surprised if you kick him again. You may want to think about investing in a leash.

******

My friend Scottie the "Whore" always gets the girls, while I'm left holding his beer. What am I doing wrong?

— *Ben*

Holding his beer. That's what you're doing wrong Ben.

******

So, whatever happened to the other guy, the girl, and the pizza place?

— *HB in MI*

The girl, lovely Traylor Howard, went on to play Layla Baileygates in *Me, Myself & Irene*. The other guy, Richard Ruccolo, continued his career in such movies as *Anacardium* and *All Over the Guy*. Then, in October of 2001, Ruccolo proved successful in love as well, announcing his engagement to Tiffani Amber-Thiessen.

Alas, the pizza place has not fared so well. Dropped from the title of the show in the third season, "Beacon Street Pizza" became increasingly filled with self-doubt. When the show was finally cancelled, the pizza place blamed itself, wondering why it hadn't been cast as that always-successful venue, a coffee house.

Its confidence shattered, "Beacon Street Pizza" fell into a downward spiral of one desperate reinvention after another. The turn of the millennium saw the pizza place in such unlikely roles as "Beacon Street Beanery," and "Beacon Street Papaya King," culminating in the poorly received pilot attempt, *Two Arabs, a Jew and a Falafel Shack.*

******

My friend and I are arguing over who gives the better blowjob. I mean, we both suck, use our tongues, swallow and always remember to play with the balls, so it's hard to determine without a volunteer… we were wondering if you'd settle the debate for us. What do you say?
— *VansFav*

That's it. I've had enough of these gag questions. I'm trying to run a serious advice column here, Mom.

******

dear van,,,, im curious about certian things and im hoping you could answer. is it true that beer before licquire gets you drunk quicker? thank you for your time and hopefully you will answer my questions.
— *natasha, montreal, canada*

Before I address the multitudinous spelling and punctuation errors in your query, let me first take a sip of water. Ok. Obviously you have no CAPS LOCK button. Fine. I accept that. And maybe you're even missing the apostrophe key. Possibly. Not likely, but I'll let it slide. Your comma key is working overtime at the beginning of your letter, which is good. If commas don't get enough exercise they get fat and lazy and mean spirited. Much like the Swedes. Is "licquire" a kind of "liqueur?" A kind of Kahlua, perhaps? If you know, I'm "certian" you'll tell me.

Ah, now, you had a question, didn't you? "Beer before liquor" will get you drunk quicker. It will also get whatever you've eaten that day to pay a visit to your esophagus, throat, mouth, and linoleum, in that order.

I'm trying to decide where to go to college, where do you recomend?
— *Ali*

The Spelling Academy of ANYWHERE. In fact, invite Natasha to go with you.

******

Is it just me or is *Clockstoppers* just a rip off of a *Ducktales* episode? Do you remember when Huey, Duey, and Louie had a clock made by Gyro that would slow down time? Remember how they foiled the Beagle Boys? They did it in episode #026 called "Time Teasers" that originally aired March 4, 1988.
— *Lance*

Thank God someone else sees it too! Of course I remember that episode. I will never forget the look on the collective Beagle Boys' faces when they realized that once again, they had been outsmarted by those magnificent mallards.

In a similar vein, you must also have seen the overwhelming parallels between that one Dilbert comic strip where Dilbert gets assigned to this impossible project by his pointy-haired boss who is just sooooooo clueless, and the way John Proctor, in Arthur Miller's *The Crucible*, grabs Abigail by her hair and calls her a whore, before finally admitting his own affair. I'm glad I've finally found somebody on the same wavelength. Thanks again Lance.

THE CRUCIBLE
BY
ARTHUR MILLER

******

How am I supposed to have sex if my roommate never leaves our dorm room?
— *Kim*

Tsk. Tsk, Kim. Have you never heard of sharing? Life is more fun when you're inclusive, not exclusive. Ask your roommate to join in and the whole world smiles with you. Unless of course, you're a Korean man looking for hot bi-action, in that case the world averts its eyes in horror, so maybe you should rent a motel.

******

What's the deal with these lions trying to attack us?
— *Bryana*

I know exactly what you mean, Bryana. These ferocious felines pose a menace to us all. Unfortunately, apex predators aren't easy to get rid of. The African lion can weigh up to 550 pounds and achieve a top speed of 40 miles per hour. What hope can any human have against such a killing machine? Fortunately, we have use of our most precious weapon, the human mind.

Simply by airlifting in Kodiak bears, our lion problem could soon be solved. Weighing in at over 1400 pounds and 11 feet tall, and sporting the largest fangs of any carnivore, the Kodiak bear should have no problem with the so-called "King of Beasts." But what do we do once the bears rule the earth?

Once again, our intellect provides a solution! By creating giant "Mecha-Gorillas," complete with laser eyes, missile fingers, infrared target acquisition capabilities and armor-plated skin, we should soon rid the world of Ursus Arctos Horribilis. But at what price? For how can we deal with lumbering cyber-primates programmed solely for destruction?

A call out to space, perhaps? The Search Extra-Terrestrial Intelligence program has by now undoubtedly made contact with the Telekinetic Medullans of Regulon 5. The powerful psychic hammers wielded by these ultra-evolved aliens would soon pulverize the rampaging mecha-gorillas to powder. Alas, the obvious result of this shift in the balance of power would be the complete and utter enslavement of the human race, with all mankind working endless shifts in Nevada's borax mines.

Indeed, the only thing that stops this from happening today is the Medullans' love of relaxing in the tall grass of the hot savannas. A slow moving race, reputed to taste like gazelle, they are easy prey to those well-camouflaged masters of the hunt, the lion. Let's just let the kitties live and let live, shall we? Because otherwise we're in a war we can't win.

******

I find the expression "Naked as a Jay bird" stupid. It would make more sense to compare your nakedness to an animal without feathers or hair or anything. Maybe one of those ugly hairless cats for example. What do you think?
— JohnS

Interesting point, John, but the expression derives from the phrase "naked as Jay Byrd." Originally coined by Connecticut third graders in the year 1980, the phrase pertained to one Jay Byrd, a troubled youth who smelled of incense and Fritos, but who won everlasting fame for his habit of running naked through the streets of Stamford. In a similar vein, the phrase "dumb as Mark Sapperstein" is also eponymous. Even though the expression never caught the popular imagination, man was that kid dumb.

******

I was at a pre-Spring Break party last week and a guy told me I had drank too much. I was offended, deeply. So much that my deep-seated, guttural hurt liberated itself onto his shoes. I then head-butted him, took his beer, and grabbed some girl. Do you think that made me appear to be insensitive?
— Baxter

Vomiting? Head-butting? Unsolicited fondling? Where to start, where to start? I know! How about Junior College? A Junior College for a junior party-goer. Good God, Baxter! I'm so mad I almost want to admonish you. But I won't. Because at least you were smart enough to take the beer. You almost ruined a perfectly good party. In my book, that's a big N. And a big O. Know what that spells? KARMA. I'm disappointed Baxter. The only credo of mine you did follow was "Don't be a fool, leave them your stool." But that one's way down on the list. Way, way down.

******

Where in the world is Carmen Sandiego?
— *McElmurry*

Ah, the "where are they now" question that plagues the celebrity-obsessed. Very well... After a long run on PBS, success went to Carmen Sandiego's head. She started spending less and less time committing capers throughout the globe, and more and more time in "the Holiday Shores Motel" in Hollywood, California.

It was there that she settled into a bleak routine of "huffing" wart remover fluid and listening to 12" Rockapella Remixes. Her marriage to George Michael brought her a brief respite from her twin demons of ether-based inhalants and all-male a cappella groups, but within months it became clear that union was ill-fated, as both parties found themselves bumping into each other in Beverly Hills restrooms.

Things briefly looked better for Carmen in 1998, when she signed to co-host an "Ab Slider" infomercial with Chuck Norris. Unfortunately, the deal fell through after she was caught stealing Norris's copper healing bracelet. "Once an international jewel thief, always an international jewel thief," shrugged the martial arts superstar. But the bottom is rubber for Carmen. Fox Networks has recently signed her for the revamped "Celebrity Boxing VI." She is currently slated to fight Kim Fields ("Tootie" from *Facts of Life*.)

******

How do you tell your girlfriend that she has a bush the size of a rainforest? More importantly, how do I get rid of the damn thing (the hairy bush, not my girlfriend)
— *Ken*

Be careful what you wish for, Ken. It might come true. Remember that rainforests are invaluable ecosystems, home to millions of rare species, with their dense foliage serving as the lungs of the world. God forbid the shaving process begin! Do you really want Sting, Peter Gabriel, and the Indigo Girls holding a $300 a plate dinner protesting you, Ken?

******

My sorority sisters and I are planning a sleepover party. Do you have any suggestions of what we can do for fun besides drink?
— *Sister XOXO's*

I know what you can do for fun... HOW ABOUT NOT GETTING MURDERED?! DOES THAT SOUND LIKE FUN?! Whatever happens, make sure that you and your sexy young sorority sisters don't frolic in your bras and panties, while a panting, deranged psycho-killer watches you through the window.

DO NOT start talking about the myth of the deranged psycho-killer who stalks the campus every April 5th, looking for unsuspecting co-eds to slaughter. (ESPECIALLY don't do that if your sleepover is on April 5th!!!) And, for God's sake, if you hear any strange noises, don't go investigate one at a time... unless you WANT your pretty little heads being used as horrific art-deco accent pieces inside a deranged psycho-killer's shack. Other than that, cribbage, or the titillating "truth or dare," can be terrific sleepover activities. Have fun!

Where can I buy a cheap monkey?

— *Matt*

Where can't you buy a cheap monkey? Since the phrase "A monkey in the hand is worth two in the bush" is in vogue again, monkey stores have been springing up all over. Why I live next door to no less than four monkey stores: The Monkey Connection, Monkeyrama, Victoria's Monkey, and the monkey-themed restaurant Monkey's!

Sorry, I'm kidding. To be honest, I don't know. Try Canada.

******

Who da' man?

— *Bob*

I did a little research on this, Bob, and quite frankly I was surprised with the results. According to all reputable experts, and Ask Jeeves, da' man is actually Christopher Hewitt, TV's "Mr. Belvedere."

******

Did you take a shit on my rug?

— *Mr. Pooper*

Why? Is one missing? Ha ha ha ha ha ha ha ha! Sorry. The answer: no. Just Curious, do you know someone named Baxter?

******

Do you kiss my mother with that mouth?!

— *Chris M*

Chris, Chris, Chris, Chris, Chris, Chris, Chris. Your mother, like all ladies of the evening, will do most anything for a price. Golden showers. Brown showers. Roman showers. Why she would do things that would make Caligula blush. But kiss? I think not. There are some things that money just can't buy. By the way, tell her I said hi, and I'll bring back that thing on Monday. I washed it. ;)

******

Is it wrong to mix sex and cheese?
— *Micky (aka: The Hoof)*

Only if it's goat cheese; and only if it's still inside the goat when you're doing the "mixing." But I have a hunch that anyone nicknamed "The Hoof" would already know a thing or two about that subject, wouldn't they? If a little voice inside you says it's wrong, then it's probably wrong. Moreover, if a little voice pinned underneath you says, "it's wrong" then it's definitely wrong.

******

Did you take my wallet?
— *Max*

There's only one way to be certain, Max. One month from now, look at the charges on your credit card bill. If there aren't any charges for Llama rentals, dry ice, fog machines, topless Mariachi bands, a troop of dancing animatronic polar bears and penguins, or 50,000 pomegranates, you can be relatively sure it wasn't me.

******

My university campus over here in Germany is about to go belly up because they don't have the money. What is the proper etiquette for this situation?

— *Ace*

Etiquette schmetiquette! You gotta save the campus, Ace! You and your small but loyal group of misunderstood friends are the only thing standing in the way of the conniving Kaiser Von Assmunscher's evil scheme to turn the University into a Bavarian amusement park.

You have to come up with a zany plan that'll never work. Then with some hard work, ingenuity, and a little bit of luck culminating in a major party, you and your friends will almost certainly succeed against all odds. Just don't forget to engage in tons of hilarious hijinks along the way! It's all up to you, Ace. You have to save the university, publicly humiliate the antagonistic Kaiser, and get the girl. What are you still doing here? Get going!

******

Where is "the Love"?

— *David*

Did you check the pockets of the pants you were wearing yesterday?

******

What is the better pickup line: "I go to Harvard Law School" or "I graduated from Oxford?" Or should I just buy her drinks until she doesn't know the difference?

— *Jonathan*

In your case, it sounds like a better pick up line would be "Hey, I have self-esteem issues. Heal me." But, hey! Why limit yourself here, Jonathan? Use 'em all! Pickup lines are just like cologne – the more you use, the better. Is it too far-fetched to hope a girl believes that you're going to Harvard Law School after graduating from Oxford? I think not. On the other hand, buying her plenty to drink won't hurt either.

******

Last night happened to be my twentieth birthday. In an effort to get laid I drank one too many forties. I woke up in a laundry basket magic-markered from toe to ear. What is the best way to remove the permanent marker?
— *JohnW.*

Do you know of the Naga people, or of their ancient tribal custom of tattoos? I guess not. Well here's a little NAGA 101: you see, most of the Naga live in India in the states of Manipur and Arunachal Pradesh. Here's the good news. Women do not cover their breasts. The bad news, John? Well, the men's tattoos indicate their status in their tribe, and depending on the marker tattoos you received, you may be considered a "devil man." John, are you a Devil Man? Check. Find a mirror. Open your eyes. PERCEIVE!!

If you have exchanged your soul with an angry demon's, then don't worry about the tats. Worry about the eternal wheel of pain and suffering known as Samsara. If you aren't a Devil Man, well, I don't know what will take it off. Have you tried an ice cream scoop?

******

If I rub enlarging cream on my dick, won't my hand get bigger?
— *Shmuckboy*

A very clever observation Shmuckboy, verging on the droll, but you miss a far more important fact. If you rub enlarging cream on your penis, and then engage in intercourse, your partner's vagina will also enlarge, thereby necessitating the application of more cream to your member, which in turn will cause a bigger vagina. Such an endless cycle might well lead the two of you to have sexual organs big enough to blot out the rays of the sun, thus destroying life as we know it here on Earth. So please, shmuckboy, stick to regular hand lotion.

******

Is sex really better if you're moving at the speed of light?
— *Logan*

No. But it will appear so to observers here on Earth. Don't forget - Time and Speed are relative. An erotic encounter at warp factor one may only feel like two minutes to you, Speed Racer, but by the time it's over, most of your friends at mission control will be dead of old age.

******

What's shakin'?
— *Groove Nation*

What isn't shakin', groove nation? That's the better Q. Everything's shakin' including the pillar on which I've built all my beliefs. Last week I threw a party for a girl and didn't even get a phone call after. Played all the right music, poured all the right drinks. I even sang the last five verses of "Hotel California" to her.

Whoa. I can't believe I actually just wrote those words. I think maybe my brain has consumption. Cough cough. I hope. Well, clearly, that was the problem. HOTEL CALIFORNIA? What was I thinking? Probably not a lot. Thank you, Groove Nation, for giving me the hindsight to see my own folly. Bless you, and your country of groove citizens.

Groove on.

******

Is it wrong to have sex with a dwarf or a midget without a video camera?

— *Tin Man*

You ask two very different questions, Tin Man. While both dwarves and midgets are "little people," they are hardly the same. You see, TM, "Dwarfism" is defined as short stature, 4 feet 10 inches or less, as the result of a medical or genetic condition. There are more than 200 different types of dwarfism, many of which have not been defined by medical science. There are an estimated 100,000 dwarves living in the United States (indeed, one might say, a small army). Most dwarves have "normal" sized heads and torsos, but small arms and legs.

A "midget," however, is the term used for a proportionate dwarf. The term has fallen into disfavor in recent times and is considered offensive by most people of short stature. Such terms as dwarf, little person, LP, and person of short stature are all acceptable, but most people would rather be referred to by their name than by a label. But I digress. The short answer to your first question is: it's up to you. And the answer to your second question is: yes, it would be wrong. You should always have a video camera handy whenever you have sex. Remember to get signed waivers.

******

Recently, I succumbed to an irresistible urge to mail Martha Stewart a dead bird. According to to FedEx, she should receive it no later than 3:00 p.m. Monday. What should I expect to happen next?

— *Max*

Look for an attractively-framed restraining order to arrive in your mail sometime within the week.

******

My wheelbarrow has a squeaky wheel. I've tried a few lubes, but nothing seems to work. I know a squeaky wheel doesn't seem like a big deal, but on campus I'm a practical joker who likes to sneak up on people. I guess I should mention that I have elephantitis and I use the wheelbarrow to push around my left nut. What type of oil do you recommend to get rid of my squeak?
— *Squeaky and not-so sneaky*

3-in-1.

I wanted to impress this great-looking girl, so I told her I was an eighth-level mage and invited her out to our weekly D & D meeting. She laughed in my face, called me a geek and walked away. What should I do?
— *Gandalf*

Well, Gandalf, sounds like you need to re-roll the old twenty-sided charisma dice and pray for doubles. You might want to invest in a +2 cologne as well.

******

Who in God's name are you? And after I know WHO you are, WHY in God's name would I ask you even one simple question for you to answer? Answer me that! Thanks.
— *Jimbo*

Who am I? Who am I indeed. I am many things to many people. To the Penobscot Indian, I am the Spirit of the Salmon. To the Yamamano of the Amazon basin, I am the Jaguar King. To Billy Parker, I'm known as Van Wiffer.

I remember it as if it were yesterday. Parker on second. Strebowski on Third. Little Ronnie Reed was on the mound. I owned Reed that season, but it was the playoffs. Was Reed sandbagging all year for just this moment? I say yes. But to Parker, he'll always be stranded on second.

Let it go, Parker. Let it go.

Will this really make me go blind?

— *Eric C.*

Before you go checking yourself into the Braille Institute, Eric, let's clarify what you mean by "this." If by "this" you mean staring directly into the solar eclipse that will be visible in Western Angola on December 4 of this year, then my answer will have to be in the affirmative. Yes, this activity could cause permanent vision loss. But only if you refuse to wear the proper eye protection.

However, if by "this" you mean setting your DVD player on repeat and watching the latest Girls Gone Wild video for 17 continuous hours this weekend, you have nothing to worry about. Your peepers will be just fine. However, you should invest in a Norelco for those paws of yours. You're bound to start sprouting palm-bush any second now.

******

I threw a brunch party last week for the 50th anniversary of my school's marching band, and no girls came. What should I have done?

— *Big Brass*

Wow. Where to start? Because my space here is limited to less than 70 pages of text, I can't really tell you everything you need to know. So here's the condensed version, instruments: metal guitar, sax or drums only. (Also, never call a harmonica a mouth harp in front of girls). Parties: brunch? No college party should ever have poached eggs or salmon mouse as part of the menu. And 12 noon? Midnight yes, Noon no. Anniversaries: try again at the centennial. Bring fireworks.

******

Would I be committing any grievous social faux pas by using Gary Coleman's butt for a bicycle rack? And if not, what's a fair price to pay for this service?
— *No Kick-Stand*

Yes, it would be wrong. Very wrong. Don't you think Gary Coleman has suffered enough in his short life? (No pun intended... ok, I intended it, but it was just a little joke. Oops! Sorry.) Anyway, you may or may not be aware that Mr. Coleman has undergone three operations for a congenital kidney defect known as nephritis. As a result of this condition he will never grow any taller than 4 foot 8 inches in height.

Not to mention, after playing Arnold Drummond on the extraordinarily popular comedy series *Diff'rent Strokes* (1978-1986) Coleman wound up faced with not only the uncertainty of life as a former child star, but also he became the central character in a bitter legal squabble between himself and his parents, before finally ending up as a security guard. So shame on you for even asking! Should you choose to ignore my advice, however, his going rate is $32.50 per hour.

******

Mr. Wilder, I don't know where my shoes are. Do you?
— *Peener*

Ahh, Peener. Peener, Peener, Peener, Peener, Peener, Peener, Peener. Peeeeener. Peeee-heee-heee-heeener. Peener. Mmmm. No, I don't know where they are. Peener.

******

I met this supermodel at a frat party last night, but when I woke up this morning there was an ugly girl in my bed. What happened?
— NPS

Congratulations, NPS. You actually did have sex with a supermodel. It's a little-known fact that real supermodels take great pains to conceal their true identities lest they give away their whereabouts to super villains. It's only thanks to your date's thick glasses and her fifty-pound ass mold that you didn't wake up in the morning fighting Doctor Octopus.

******

My boyfriend showed me a website featuring "Ponygirls." They are women wearing leather harnesses and bridles pulling men around on carts. Do you know anything about the origin of Ponygirls? Is it worth exploring?
— EvieLaStrange

I'm sorry, Evie, but I don't really have a clue about "Ponygirls." How could I know anything about leather-clad women champing at their bridles as they pull their master's sulky across the show ring, their bodies quivering at the lightest touch of the riding crop? And where would I  possibly have learned about the intricacies of human dressage? Do you think that I am the kind of person who subscribes to "Equus Eroticus?" No, Evie, the world of ponygirl training is a complete and utter mystery to me.

******

How do I stop my Dad from hitting on my roommates?
— *T.C.*

Why stop him? We all have needs, and if the only thing your folks are sharing is a cup of divorce or a spoonful of celibacy then why don't you turn the other cheek and help your dad try to turn a few cheeks too? You two can bond, hug, cry, who knows...

Otherwise, you can just wait for your roommates to tell your dad he's creepy. Shouldn't take longer than twenty minutes.

******

Am I too young to have a goiter?
— *Kid with a Second Head Growing Out of his Throat*

Everybody's too young to have a goiter, KWASHGOOHT. Unless you're in the circus. Are you in the circus? Picture this - The Amazing Goiter Boy! Ka-ching! Cash cow, that's all I'm saying. No, seriously, are you in the circus? I need a bearded lady for a thing I'm throwing next week. I told the people coming it's BYOBearded lady, but you know how it is. No one listens. Circus freaks don't grow on trees. Except for Sycamora, Queen of the Forest. Write that down.

******

Will listening to Enya get me kicked out of my frat house?
— *I Love Enya!!!!!*

No. Listening to Enya will get you beaten to death with your own leg. In fact, write that down too.

******

Is spending a decade in college a bad thing?
— *Still undecided*

In the great tradition of Chinese philosophy, I'm going to answer your question with a question. So let me ask you this, Father Time... where do you have to be in such a hurry? SU, let me share a secret with you. Life is a river, a big river. A big wet river we're all crowd-surfing down. – Trite but true. Listen, your only job on this river is to relax and let it take you to, well, to wherever the river dumps you out. Veer right at the fork or you'll end up in upstate New York. Hope not. I'm rooting for you.

******

What number of phone calls constitutes stalking?
— *Linked by Destiny to Enya!!!*

Let's define "stalking." The dictionary defines stalking as a verb meaning "to pursue quarry or prey stealthily." It then defines quarry as "an open excavation usually for obtaining building stone, slate, or limestone." So don't chase rocks or wear army fatigues, and you should have no trouble with the law. Keep calling. Or better yet, go with the reverse psychology approach instead. Put a restraining order on her! Do your best to never see her again. It'll drive her crazy. Women always want what they can't have. Never forget that. In fact, write that down.

******

It's my first semester in college and I hate it here! Hate it! I find myself drawing up elaborate plans detailing how I am going to execute everyone in my class! What should I do?
— *Will S.*

Whoa! Stop right there, William! Killing sprees are soooooooooo high school. Time to turn that frown upside down. You're in college now! Why not join an extra-curricular club? In your case, perhaps the Marilyn Manson Role-play Group, or a drum circle. Just stay away from school council. It's a nest of vipers in there!

******

Enya! Enya! Enya!
— *The Future Mr. Enya!!!*

All right! That's enough! That's not even a question.

Students Rally to Save Van Wilder's Ride

— Courtesy, The Coolidge College Liberator

Students are rallying to support Coolidge senior Van Wilder since his personal transit device came under fire last Tuesday. The complaint, filed by Professor McDoogle of the Economics Department, claims that the customized golf cart, which is owned and operated by Wilder, poses numerous health and safety risks to students and faculty on campus. The professor's complaint calls for the immediate confiscation and removal of the vehicle from campus by the Office of Public Safety.

Van Wilder's publicity office has offered no official comment on the matter. However, dozens of student groups and clubs on campus have come out in support of Wilder and his personalized cart. The students say that Professor McDoogle's claims are false. "McDoogle is lame," stammered one supporter at Friday night's Beer Bong for Justice Event sponsored by the Pneumatics Society, "Van Wilder is the raddest [expletive] dude alive."

Other campus groups are planning pro-Wilder events as well. The Intramural Topless Table Tennis Association in conjunction with the Co-Ed Nerf & Jell-O Sports Organization plans to hold a Nerf Frisbee Tournament this Saturday at 2 p.m. at Kinsey Field. The Disabled Student Union plans to hold a "freedom ride" through Sweeny Square next Tuesday at 4 p.m. to show their support for Wilder.

The Office of Public Safety refused to comment on the Wilder dilemma. However, The Liberator did get one officer to go on record regarding the event. Officer Rupert Finklestein said that Wilder's cart, which he received last month as a gift from the Golf Team Booster Club, had every legal right to operate on campus.

"Prior to presenting Mr. Wilder with the cart, the GTBC filled out the proper paperwork and collected the required 2,700 student signatures needed to receive a Class B on-campus driving permit. Mr. Wilder's cart is completely sanctioned for use within the boundaries of the Coolidge campus," Officer Finklestein said.

"I'd also like to go on record saying that Van has used his cart to provide many altruistic services on campus. He started the Ride-With-Dignity program that offers free and confidential rides home to the students after one-night stands that result in 'walks of shame' and provided free shuttle service for the Divorced Mothers group during last fall's Parents' Week."

As of press time, Professor McDoogle had not returned any of The Liberator's telephone calls.

NATIONAL PARTY
SCHOOL RANKING

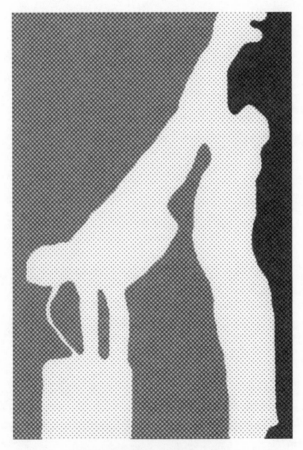

ACCORDING TO
MIIIIIATCH

Miiiiiatch's
Party School Ranking

There are times in life when you meet someone who is a kindred spirit. There is something about them, the look they give you sets you on your heels, maybe their aura is the right shade of chartreuse, or something like that. Whatever it is, the signal is clear from the start: this person is going to have an impact on you. Mitch was not one of these people. I should rephrase that; Mitch was not immediately one of these people.

When I first met Mitch he was face down in a sea of empty PBR cans. It was 4:45 in the afternoon. The first words I heard come out of his mouth were, "*Hmmmmm, augggggggh, errrrr. Ha, ha, ha.*" – scintillating. In fairness, since at that point we rolled him into a corner of the backyard, I did not actually "meet" Mitch until later that evening. I was throwing a little soiree. It was nothing special, just something I put together between breaking bread at Hillel House and cutting catfish at the African American Club during Stereotypical Celebrations and Ethnic Week.

I say it was nothing special... that is until Mitch came to life around 6:30. He was visiting some friends at Coolidge so he'd only been in town for a few days but he already had an impressive posse who he called, upon regaining consciousness. To mark each of their arrivals (and several times during the night) a cheer went up for *Miiiiiatch!* The boy could get things going. It sure made my job easier. I'm relatively sure that if you Google the phrase, "do not try this at home" you will see a picture of Mitch and his friends. They rocked hard, they partied hard, and the slept... well I'm not sure how they slept, but I've heard stories.

Speaking of stories, Mitch told me he was on a mission. The mission was to assemble the greatest college party school ranking of all time. The idea was a simple one: Mitch would visit schools he'd heard about, Mitch would party, Mitch would write about his experiences, and move on to the next school on the list.

"One thousand schools, man. In one year!" He said before being interrupted by his cell. The ensuing conversation consisted entirely of the word dude. "Dude, dude, d.o.o.o.o.o.o.d, dude, etc. etc." Then, turning to me, he said, "dude." And I knew exactly what he meant. When I told him about the *Van Wilder Guide To Graduating College In Eight Years Or More*, he wanted to know if I could help get his party school ranking published. So I said that it'd be great to see what he came up with and I'd put him in touch with my people.

The next day, he sent me ten great articles about some schools that sounded like a lot of fun, but I haven't heard from him since. Did he ever visit all one thousand schools? Where did Coolidge rank? Did he ever settle that paternity suit?

Like I said, "do not try this at home…" or in your dorm, or anywhere for that matter, because you are not Miiiiiatch. It's possible that even Mitch is no longer Miiiiiatch, but my guess is he's still out there somewhere doing his "research."

ARIZONA STATE

#5

Welcome to the desert. Arizona is one of the hottest damn places in the US, and Arizona State is located in the heart of it. When you think blistering heat, cactus, and dying of dehydration, Arizona State should be in your thoughts. Although being hotter than a layer of hell, Arizona State makes for some damn good partying. The ladies here are some of the hotter ones I've seen… with their sexy tans and ability to drink more than most men I know.

On my trip to Arizona I got there later on in the day, so my buddy Robbie was already trashed. I knew this because one eye was completely shut and he kept asking me, "Where all the bitches at?" My answer all 14 times was, "I don't know dickface, you're the one who lives here." There were two girls at his place, but I guess they just didn't tickle his fancy, even though I have this photograph of him with one of them… Drunk people are notorious for their special vision, or lack thereof, and Robbie is no different.

Eventually he got enough sense to tell me there was a badass sports bar we could go to, called McDuffys. I'm more of a house party guy but, you say, "sports bar" and I can't resist. Big-ass TVs, the smell of fresh beer, wood-covered interior… It brings a tear to my eye, and a sticky drizzle down my leg.

We showed up and the place was pretty mellow, and had a sh*tload of TVs. The waitresses were hot, and skanky, which is always good. We bought a couple beers, but it wasn't really working for me. Robbie was pretty incoherent so even a Port-o-Potty party would've worked for him. I thought about how to get out of there smoothly, but I knew the only way to get him to leave would be vagina. Therefore I sucked it up and hit on some girls with my unbelievable "hitting on girls" skills. A wing man is always handy, but because Robbie was out of commission I went in solo. Like any gentleman, I asked the bartender for three of the cheapest mixed drinks they served, left no tip, and brought 'em to the girls table. It was asshole-tastic.

Of course when I got to the table I received the, "what the hell does this guy want" face, but when I said I worked for a magazine and I'm looking for the hottest girls of Arizona State— BAM! I was gold. Through little conversation I found out there was a big-ass house party about two blocks away. My face lit up with joy, but before the girls had even taken two sips off their drinks, Robbie stumbled over and very loudly yelled, "You found the bitches!!" Before my head could hit the table in embarrassment, the girls were already leaving. They were so disgusted they just left, and took the drinks I just paid for. One of them even got a little "sassitude" and did the head shake-finger snap, which made my heart hurt oh so much more.

Yet one of the very few good things about having a really drunk friend is: they basically don't care about anything. By not caring, I mean he quickly grabbed his balls, flipped her off and called her a wench. Not my exact expectations; I expected more from some one as drunk as Rob, but hey it was still entertaining. Robbie went on to tell me about a place called "Mill Avenue" which is basically the "Bourbon Street of Arizona." It sounded appealing, but it was a long ways away.

This woman debacle was devastating but the night was not lost, because we still had the house party. I told Robbie, and despite not getting vagina for him, we took off. Outside there were people wandering around all over, it was pretty cool. For some reason Robbie threw on sunglasses, at 11:00 p.m. He told me, "It looks cool," and I of course told him he looked like a jackoff.

The pad we were going to had people all over the place, front yard, side yard, street, cars, and yes, the roof. The roof guys looked to be getting stoned out of their minds, and I'm sure they had a lot of fun getting down. When we got inside, neither of us knew anyone. But someone ran up to us with a beer bong three steps inside, and did the whole, "WOOOO... BEER BONG!" thing. I of course got into it and yelled the same. For some reason it was dark beer, making it all the more intoxicating. He handed it to Robbie, and my good ol' pal says, "You need to catch up Mitch." I gotta catch up with a damn dark beer bong?!... *Super*. So without much hesitation I slam it down.

When I come back up, I get all the taste and realize something wasn't right. But before I could get the whole thought together in my head, the random guy yells, "DUDE there was four shots of Jack Daniels, and a Natty Ice in there." DARK BEER MY ASS!! Now realizing I may black out or yack at any moment, I slap the beer bong across Robbie's face knocking his sunglasses crooked, which the son of a bitch deserved.

Ten minutes rolled by and I was trashed. Surprisingly, I held in the throat juice and then me and Rob went to town on the party. The girls there were awesome, they were down for it all. I saw girls making out, rubbin' boobs, doing shots through boobs, I thought I had found paradise.  Then when some other chick realized all the boob action was happening and other girls were getting all the attention she walked up to me, and said, I sh*t you not, "I bet my cooter would get the attention off them." Thinking I was about to see some bald nooner I quickly reached for the camera, but it stayed PG-13 and it was just underwear for me. Yet it was still a girl lifting her skirt up for me… so I still felt like a winner.

 I saw bulge, so she had some bush down there, and I'm a bald guy myself. After the photography she gave me the wide mouth gasp, like I was an asshole or something. But I know for a fact she loved it. Either way she went back to talking to some chicks and I went mingling. The party raged on and me and my pal Robbie got pretty destroyed. Robbie actually ended up taking someone's army jacket, and I peed on a radio. It was faaaantastic. By 3:00 a.m. the party was still an actual party, and not just a bunch of sloshed people trying to get some action.

Except for me, I was very sloshed and because the girl who showed me the panties was top notch, I couldn't resist. I went back to her to work the suave drunken magic and got an invitation to her place. Before I went I took one last picture of me and Robbie, and it's one of the drunker ones I've seen.

All in all Arizona State surpassed my expectations. I only knew my buddy Robbie but there were hot woman down for anything all over the place, beer flowed like water, and I got trashed in record time. Not to mention the little red  panties girl slobbed my garbage. So I give Arizona State 7 out of 10 keg stands and 5 out of 5 pairs of boobs. The women were hot, crazy, and alcoholics. I couldn't get enough of 'em, but the alcohol was a little pricey at the sports bar, and I didn't see too many liquor stores with cheap prices. But at the house party it was all free, so it still works for me. Cheers to Arizona State.

UNIVERSITY OF NEVADA LAS VEGAS

#22

When running through the fluff introduction to a campus, you come across some pretty heavy winded bullsh*t. Yet, there were none quite like the information given by the University of Nevada Las Vegas' website, which read as follows…

…Las Vegas is a city with many exciting attractions. Like any other large metropolitan area, the city has fine libraries, museums, community-theater, art galleries, and parks, which are enjoyed and supported by more than one million local residents. As one of the fastest-growing areas in the United States, southern Nevada is an example of modern urban living…

Wow! How about jerkin' me off a little more?! Libraries!? Museums?! In all of your life, whether through experience or watching a movie about Vegas, have you *EVER* heard someone say anything remotely close to, "Hey guys let's go hit the f#@kin museum! WOOO!" No… no you haven't, and completely avoiding the fact that the college is in the left ventricle of the heart of Las Vegas makes it scarier to parents than actually having the information in there.

I've made the trip to Las Vegas a few times now, for gambling, good times, and prostitutes… lots, and lots… of prostitutes. This place is f#@king fantastic… Alcohol is available 24 hours a day, clubs and bars never close, the party never stops. The cops basically don't give a sh*t because everything's legal… and noise violations?? – More rare then my sobriety.

With a school three minutes away from the Las Vegas strip... how in the living hell can you not have it be a top party school? More than being so close to total insanity, greed, lust, gluttony, and basically every sin possible, you've got special protection in good ol' Vegas. Protection like open alcohol containers being legal everywhere... even the backseat of a moving vehicle doing 95 on the 505 Freeway. You may get nailed for speeding, but feel free to pass around the shot glasses when the cop walks up... 'CAUSE IT'S LEGAL!!!

So the pre-party doesn't all have to be in the dorm room, or your buddy's apartment. You can slam shots while someone drives your ass to the bars, clubs, and casinos. Although a pre-party bonanza of speedy alcohol consumption is always good times, as Vegas resident and my good buddy, Kevin Rogers, shows you here with a double shot of tequila and then a jumping 180 scissor kick.

With prostitution and stripping being a nice large chunk of the Vegas economy the chances of not getting laid are almost non-existent. 'Cause no matter what, you're getting drunk... and when you're drunk, everyone wants some vagina, and money comes out of your wallet effortlessly... unless you suffer from whiskey dick... (my cold-blooded adversary for many years). So if you've got 35 dollars, and the capacity to dial an 800 number for whores... then you, my friend, can get laid.

Vegas wants you drunk, because "you drunk = money for them." So free alcohol is in abundance at most casinos. This is why whenever I see the old cocktail waitress walking towards me I quickly pull out a quarter, slap it in a slot machine and then they offer me free booze, 'cause they think I'm gambling. Hey, if you think that's wrong, you're a moron. You think they wouldn't take advantage of *your* drunk ass?

During my most recent trip to Vegas, I hit the strip... going up and down through clubs and bars like mad. I wouldn't suggest this on a regular basis. It's not that cheap, which is why me and my friend Kevin drank half a gallon of vodka in the back of his car before entering clubs with nine-dollar shots, and seven-dollar cups of beer. I suggest doing the drinking BETWEEN clubs, as opposed to in them.

On this trip while at Coyote Ugly, one of the oh-so-sexy bar dancing girls called me an "obnoxious asshole" 'cause I yelled out that the song they were playing "sucked my asshole." She then announced that if I had balls, I'd enter a beer drinking competition...

Let me step aside for a moment here.

A girl... who just called me an obnoxious asshole... wanted to make me look dumb by telling me to compete in beer drinking... haha... AAAAHAHAHA... HAHAHAHAHAHAHA.

Obviously, I completely f#@king *RAPED* every single person in the competition and then slammed my cup down at her feet. This was followed by her saying, "That was the fastest I've ever seen anyone drink a beer." So my reward was a little kissy kiss, having her throw on some sweet ass Metallica, letting me sing some "Enter Sandman," then she poured some hard alcohol down the gullet... moments later I asked her to marry me.

So all in all... I had a damn fine Vegas time, and have had good times there every visit: lots of women, free with some effort, or pricey with no effort, alcohol everywhere, available at any time, drinkable at any place, something to do 24 hours a day, and legal gambling. This is damn near paradise. I can't imagine this kind of temptation every single day. By week three I'd look like Nicholas Cage in *Leaving Las Vegas*, and have a similar alcoholism problem.

Getting any school done... or having money left for tuition must be a difficult task every semester for students here, but goddamn it'd be a fun ride. I give it 7 out of 10 Keg stands because the price of alcohol is devastating unless you're sneaky. It's available 24 hours a day, but when you're in bars and around people the price is ridiculous. And UNLV gets 4 out of 5 pairs of boobs because even if you can't pull in some ridiculously good-looking women, you can still buy some. Las Vegas is coming in at number 22.

CHICO STATE

#15

When you try to find information on Chico State you run into lots of information on how wonderful its small city life is, and information about its parks and recreation. Yet magically, it's difficult to find out that it's been one of the top party schools in the country for three decades.

Chico can be found in the Northern Sacramento Valley about 90 miles north of Sacramento, in Butte County. Chico is a hippy's dreamland, being a completely isolated nature-land, and having one of the largest municipally owned parks in the nation. At Bidwell park you can do everything: go biking, hiking, swimming, ride horseys, and shoot heroin... there are endless options in Chico with all of its nature at your disposal.

Chico State is also home to an abundance of women and isolation from everything in the world, except alcohol, and drugs. Chico is a small town 40 miles from anything, in every direction, and there's not much to do in Chico besides get completely toasted. Getting sh*tfaced anywhere isn't too much of a problem, except the dorms. After the thirteenth alcohol related death in the dorms, eight years ago, Chico made themselves... a dry campus.

This sucks balls, but as you can see in the picture, it's all my friends... drinking... in a dorm room. Thanks for giving us the extra thrill while drinking, Chico State.

Although there's only the hang up of drinking in the dorms, you can pretty much drink anywhere else you want. When you get plastered, you can walk everywhere. Downtown is one crosswalk away from the campus, and if you live at the farthest apartment complex in Chico it's still only a fifteen-minute walk to get there. Along the way who knows what the hell will happen?

I've been asked to do a beer bong of wine, done... Had a girl lift her top up and rub my face in her fun bags, done... Seen people having sex in a parking lot, done... Met women on the way to a party who came home and played with my ding-a-ling at a later time, done... Been given a date rape drug, done. Although I wasn't raped, it was an interesting experience trying to regain my sight and consciousness for an hour. But if you're going to try and get smart and ride a bike instead of walk, watch your ass, because they give bike-riding DUIs... trust me.

Downtown is small, but filled with bars, and if the bars aren't your scene, walk just a hundred yards further and you've got the fraternity row. There are frats and houses with open parties all the time. Usually the frats and houses were cheaper, and crazier... therefore I was there most the time, unless bar sluts were on the mind. All in all, people were down to get hammered whenever and however, as you can see here with a variation of the keg stand, we intelligently call "the jungle juice stand." Basically named for us lifting our buddy upside down and plowing his face into our jungle juice made with four hard alcohols, and maybe some juice... And I think there was an apple involved somehow too.

Twenty years ago, Chico was at its prime with the infamous "Valley Days," where hundreds of people got naked, drank and swam down by a river every summer for a week. People started drinking at 6:00 a.m. on St. Patty's day. Halloween was becoming gigantic with thousands of people from outside the city coming in. You found people getting drunk, stoned or laid almost every day of the week, but over the past five years, Chico has cracked down hardcore on all the drinking holidays.

Riot police, SWAT, DUI checkpoints, and helicopters actually circle the area on Halloween. Spring break is purposefully put on three weeks ahead of time to block out St Patrick's Day, and the "Labor Day floating down the Sacramento River" party was also RAPED by bullsh*t city councilmen. Here is the actual list they displayed for the past four years in Chico on Halloween, along with a TV ad campaign on local channels...

· Extensive law enforcement presence with a zero tolerance for criminal behavior and traffic violations.
· Sobriety Check Points encompassing the westside and downtown areas.
· Downtown parking lots will be closed.
· No out-of-town guests allowed in on-campus housing at CSUC during Halloween.
· No street closures, no portable toilets, and no extra lights.
· A fine up to $1000 and 6 months in jail for public intoxication.
· A fine plus jail time, mandatory drug treatment program, and suspension of your drivers license for driving under the influence (car or bicycle). Your vehicle can be impounded.
· A fine plus having to return to Chico for community service hours for public urination.
· A fine for possession of an open container or having glass in the "no glass" zone.
· A fine plus loss of your driver's license if you are a minor caught in possession of alcohol.
· If arrested, you will go to jail.
· Fines for all traffic violations (vehicles and bicycles).

How much does that suck asshole?? Basically, the party got so good, and so big, that Chico took everything away. So some people got stabbed, and someone got sexually assaulted. You gotta break a few eggs to make an omelet, pansies. Chico also started making all incoming first-year students complete an online alcohol-abuse-prevention course. WOW, all this has been done, yet I go out any random weekend in Chico and there's still alcohol drinking madness. The biggest crackdown in Chico was on the big holidays, because people came from out of town, but because the city spent all their money stopping big holidays, they can't do sh*t any other given weekend... SO IT'S F#@KIN PARTY TIME!!

This place can barely afford a rent-a-cop on the weekends because the stupid bastards spent all the town's money on the holidays. Chico may be wounded by the man, but when all the money's gone, and the economy crumbles because the morons are getting rid of all tourism, I predict that Chico's party status will return and the school will be back in the top five. But for now, it's dropping back just outside the top ten.

7 out of 10 keg stands, and 4 out of 5 pairs of boobs for Chico State.

SAN JOAQUIN DELTA COMMUNITY COLLEGE

(*)(*) (*)(*)

#6

If you were to look up something on Delta Community College, you would more than likely come across the fact it's less than two miles away from another college. UOP, or the University of the Pacific. What you wouldn't realize is that UOP has fraternities and sororities all over the place. Because UOP is a very high priced, snobby and well-established school, you don't really get the insane partiers of some party schools, but when you mix in the futureless nut-jobs of Delta College... the party is on. This place is not a four-year college where you'd go to achieve a BA. Here at Delta Community College, lots of students just out of high school call the place 13th grade, because most of the younger students are still living with parents and taking on college like it's high school.

Delta College is in the middle of Stockton, CA., a growing city in northern California, across from two shopping malls and several businesses. The parties and insanity are not directly by the school, but scattered throughout the city, near UOP, the suburbs, or the gangsta area. On any given weekend you could be shot or stabbed in Stockton... it adds to the thrill.

On my many trips around and through Stockton, I've had some pretty insane times. The people are pretty much up for anything, from a bonfire at the end of an abandoned road, fraternity parties, to a full scale mansion party. Whatever's happening, people want to be in on it. On one particular trip, the drinking began during the day

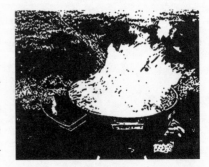

at a simple barbecue and pool party. The barbecue was started by pyromaniac extraordinaire Rob Hammerstone.

After our burgers that tasted like charcoal and lighter fluid, the drinking began in full force. Beer, liquor, and cigarettes reigned supreme. As the afternoon rolled on, some of the guys needed a little extra thrill, so they climbed up on the roof over the pool and started leaping into the water, drunk as all hell.

Once a few gainers, back flips, and cartwheels were performed for the people swimming and eating, one of the ladies felt she wasn't getting enough attention and removed her top. Much to my penis' delight. Then Steve, (my penis) was made limp when having to view my friend Russell dance around in the removed top.

The day moved on, and I struggled to bring my dong back to life, and with the heavy consumption of alcohol and energy drinks Steve, my penis, was ready for action. Once it started to get dark outside we all cleaned up and started making phone calls. We needed some ladies, some music, and some more booze, and the party was on its way.

It was about 9:00 p.m. and the party was in full force. The music was on full blast, the people were getting wild, and the ladies were looking damn good. Good enough, in fact, that I reverted back to my primal days as a caveman and picked one girl up and took her inside. What can I say, I'm an animal, yet gentle as a bear cub... ladies.

After the drinking reached critical mass around midnight it was decided that two friends had to prove their manliness by playing hand darts. To

those unfamiliar with hand darts, it involves placing your hand palm down on a dart board and then letting people hurl sharpened darts at the board until someone flinches or gets nailed with a dart. The winner is then hailed as a manly-man, and a retard.

After only three throws, my buddy Erick was nailed with a dart. He screamed in pain for moments and then sucked it up like a champion, so he was a winner in my book. Not a winner like a Lance Armstrong winner, but more like Stevie Dwimmer, Special Olympics winner from Indiana.

After hand darts, shots of liquor, and making another friend take a shot of vegetable oil, it started to get late and people were dropping out. 1:00 a.m. rolled around and good ol' Erick had just zonked out. After yelling, throwing darts at unsuspecting people and picking unprovoked fights, Erick had some payback coming to him. By 3:00 a.m. I drank myself into a blackout and don't remember the events that unfolded afterwards, I only have pictures and the flashes of what other people could remember. All I know is that going into my blackout I knew Erick had to receive punishment. Therefore Erick was no longer known as Erick, but as the Chiquita boy. With one of the finer photographs of my drunk picture taking career, I get to have a memory... of something I have no memory of.

In closing, Chiquita boy was desecrated fantastically... girls were plowed fantastically... and shots were taken fantastically. One of the top 3 hangovers of all time was experienced the next day, and it lead to blood-vessel-breaking vomiting, and the mixture of pathetic sobbing and mumbled declarations of never drinking again. I've seen, and been a part of, some of the most God-awful hangovers the likes of which no one should go through, and this was one of them. Most of the top ten hangovers of my life occurred with the Delta College partiers; they drink like parched Irishmen.

So I gotta give this place 10 out of 10 keg stands and 2 out of 5 pairs of boobs. There are some girls, but not to the extent of some schools. I think that's why the alcoholism runs rampant.

FLORIDA STATE

#3

Sunny Florida, never thought Id make it so far east, but man it's nice out here. Blue skies, and beautiful scenery, but god dammit it was so humid I stood still and I was profusely sweating. It's all right though, it made me look ruggedly handsome.

When I looked up information about the school, there was also a lot of info about the other big college and large community college close by, and I thought to myself three colleges… same vicinity, oh dear God I may lose my life. When I read up about Tallahassee I found that most students enjoy the hell out of the social life there, and almost all say they wouldn't stay after graduation because they wouldn't survive. This was a good sign.

After my arrival I made my way to my buddy Eric's place. I was so jetlagged all I wanted to do was go home and go to sleep. But when I got there, I saw an entire bathtub filled with beer. I wanted to drink it all, and then take a bath in it. But I was so tired I couldn't keep moving, so I compromised with myself and took a nap in the bathtub. I'm serious. After I woke up two hours later, half my body was numb from ice, and uncomfortable-ness… but I would not leave my precious drink of the gods untouched. I got up, changed my soggy clothes and got started with a game of anchorman.

First we selected teams, and as usual I was anchorman for my team. In this special version of anchorman we didn't use just beer, though. After it was decided I was anchorman, one of the asshole locals poured his margarita into the cup and said, "You better win California boy." I held back the haymaker I was about to throw and told him Florida was for homosexuals, with a room full of people from Florida… that's just how badass I am. It was a close game, back and forth, but we couldn't make it into the big glass. I was devastated, and the sh*t talking just didn't stop. So in an effort to shut them up, AND gain a little respect, I pushed out the other three guys on my team and drank the entire thing myself. Three beers and a margarita down the gullet...

I'll come clean right now and say I yacked in my mouth. My friend Eric saw the catastrophe, but I chewed it down in all its disgustingness. Little did I know that I gained a lot of respect pounding it all, some of the other guys saw the yack happen and then the chew back... and for the first time in my life, I received no words... but only applause to shocked faces. It was a proud moment in my life, and I shall compare it to my wedding day / first child's birth, etc.

After a few more basic drinking games, we tried to figure out where to go, and by this point I was pretty gone, and I was up for anything. So without even realizing it, I agreed to go to the clubs. When we got there, I was pissed and belligerent, but some chick I didn't even know paid my way so I said, "Screw it. Let's do this." We got inside, and it had been awhile since I did the club thing. It was the same sh*t... colored lights going off, sweaty as hell, every dude who knew how to dance was getting the women.

So I sat my ass at the bar and ordered an adios motherf#@ker hoping to drink until the pain went away. Yet after I sat down the cute girl that paid my way in asked me to dance, and me being the sellout to myself that I am, I agreed. I took my drink with me and basically dry humped her for five minutes. Good times, now I've got a stiffy and no place to put it. Yes I know, I'm a little whiney bitch and I should be able to have fun anywhere, but I stand by my credo, "Clubs suck un-showered ball sack."

After my second adios, my friends had to carry me out of the place. I can't say I didn't milk it so we could get the hell out of there. But this backfired and they got me back to the pad, and tried to make me stay there and go to sleep. I won't lie. I was trashed, but not pass-out trashed. They then started f#@king with me and I lost it and chucked my shoe at my friend as he was trying to take a picture of me yelling...

It hit him in the face and he then laughed at me and said we'd go back out. I was ecstatic, and apologized to my buddy for the shoe-throwing incident, and off we went. They said we were going to a place I'd like called Bullwinkle's, and by them telling me this I was already worried that they were dropping me off at a gay bar or something. Thank God, when we arrived it was the best thing ever. Hot-ass bartenders, tons of people getting trashed, a live band, I had made it.

We all wandered around in the shoulder-to-shoulder packed area, and finally found a table that people were just leaving. We got some pitchers and went to town. It was so damn awesome, because of my loud and brazen ways we got the attention of damn near half the bar. It sucked for the band because I got an assload of people to start singing "Hotel California." The band actually quit half way through the song and picked up where I got the crowd singing. Damn, I felt like the king of the world... Who has ever been able to do that?! Once we finished up the song I was getting high-fives and love from everybody. Ass pats from the ladies were in full force and I think some dude even tried... Whatever dills your pickle, buddy.

After a few more pitchers and talking with locals, we headed back to Eric's pad with a lot of people. I had a kick-ass time at Bullwinkle's and a girl under each arm when I left... Didn't know them, never seen 'em before but it was happening, and my smile hit each ear. When we got back, his place got loaded with people, and half the bathtub was still loaded with beer. It was time to consume.

I only have a small recollection of Eric's place after we left the bar, but evidently I passed out on the kitchen floor around 5:00 a.m. after the beer ran out. I only remember waking up there cold and alone, but wow was it a good time.

In the end, the people were cool as hell, the beer was everywhere and Florida State knows how to have a helluva a good time. I give Florida State 9 out of 10 keg stands because people love to drink there, love to have a good time, and are down for anything, but I've seen lower beer prices, so it keeps 'em shy of a perfect 10. As for the ladies, they were awesome. They loved to drink, loved the bars, and loved people who were cool... namely, me. So I give them 4 out of 5 pairs of boobs, because I don't believe I got any action on this trip, but I had a lot of fun with the women. Next time I'm catching a football game, I hear there's nothing like it.

FRESNO STATE

#25

As an aspiring college student, your parents may force you to wander around the Internet or check out a few pamphlets to get an idea on colleges. If you were to do something like that with Fresno State, you might find this:

California State University, Fresno goes by the nickname "Fresno State." The university is comprised of a 388-acre main campus and a 1,011-acer farm. The home of the "Bulldogs" rests at the foot of the majestic Sierra Nevada mountain range, and is surrounded by the San Joaquin Valley, which is one of the richest agricultural areas in the world...

Welcome to the real Fresno, a large metropolitan city, with a total absence of plant life, except for the ones growing in a humid closet equipped with a heat lamp. I was surprised at the lack of countryside, but everything was industrialized in Fresno. It even had the metally asphalt smell of a city. There was no wilderness to go get hammered at a bonfire, and no trees to lose the police when you're being pursued. It was upsetting, but I didn't let it stop the drinking festivities.

We began drinking with the locals and my friends attending the school at **9:00 A.M.** This was not a casual, sipping and talking of memories past... We f#@king started by pounding a beer, and then playing asshole for a straight hour. We were drinking in the Bulldog Apartments of Fresno State, where basically every resident of the complex is a college student. So there were no complaining old people or families whining about "heavy drinking" at 9:00 in the morning... it was beautiful. Within 45 minutes I had five beers in me. The other guys were right there with me. When we reached the first hour, before even breaking his bladder, my friend Erick turned around and vomited over the edge of the car where all the drinking had started.

By this time locals and other residents of the apartment complex began opening doors, and by 11:00 a.m. we had turned the Bulldog Apartments of Fresno State into a beer-guzzling barbecue. It didn't take a lot to get things started because the apartment complex was pretty condensed. So one vomit / drunken yell and out came everyone who wasn't already partying with us.

Since we positioned ourselves in the parking lot area, we had direct vision of over a dozen dirt colored apartments, landscaped with mediocre shrubbery, and more importantly ladies changing clothes. Good times.

After a hearty day of drinking, some other students living in the complex invited us to go drink and party over at their area of the apartments. Their place was in the heart of the complex as opposed to the outskirts where we began the day. This resulted in more drinking games. A favorite of many college students, we played King's Cup. Blah, blah, blah, you play and at the end some poor bastard has to pound a ridiculous sh*t-load of alcohols that have been poured into the "king's cup" throughout the game.

Erick, in the end of one game, was looking at a concoction of several delicious liquids: jungle juice, three types of beer, wine, and a loogey, which I added when he wasn't looking. In hardcore-ass games like ours, you have two minutes to drink the whole cup, or you suffer the consequences (examples include: being kicked in the balls by every player in the game, being punched in the face by the biggest guy, or receiving a twenty-second titty twister). Erick did his damndest to drink it, quickly drinking half of it and then vomiting into a conveniently placed garbage can. Surprisingly everyone found his regurgitation extremely amusing, even the attractive women who flocked over to the game to steal some of its attention. So in an effort to add to these beautiful women getting drunker, happier, and sluttier, I cheered Erick on to finish the king's cup... or I was going to punch him in the face.

Unbelievably, after sixteen plus beers throughout the day... at 8:00 p.m. out came the shot glasses. Fresno State's own E.J. Edmerson supplied the alcohol and the encouragement to drink it, i.e. "Quit being a bitchy-ass faggot and take the shot." We all did so... and Erick vomited... again.

The drinking continued on for hours until the party died down a little and everyone felt like going into chill mode... We played another game of King's Cup... I couldn't f#@king believe it, but my friend Erick was still alive, and still conscious... and he wanted to play.

We all said Erick was out this game. He protested. He got angry. Eventually we all said f#@k it, and let the guy play. Erick's grit was uncanny. The man had my respect already, but with an overachieving drinker like Erick there was no stopping him. After an hour playing with only beer... a conspiracy enveloped our little game, and with the cooperation of me, E.J., and the distraction of two girls... Erick *magically* had to pull the last king, and had to drink the king's cup... again! Erick's yack count slowly passed a dozen... and then 15... 17... These were legitimate yacks. He swallowed... tried to keep it down... but it just didn't happen. If that bastard spit out good beer, there was going to be hell to pay.

Finally at long last, Erick passed out... unluckily for him he did so with his shoes still on, and this left him fair game for any number of horrible, yet incredibly entertaining, practical jokes. Girls kept suggesting cutesy little things like putting on makeup, or pouring *water* on his face. I said, "HORSESH*T!! This young man drank himself into a coma, he deserves worse." I had my own ideas, and mine involved a hardware store industrial strength permanent marker. Without much movement... I created my masterpiece: a purple mask complete with a skin colored penis on his forehead. With the always appropriate sentence of "I'm Gay" on his neck.

Note: (This ink did not completely come off Erick for 3 days)

After the artwork, I continued drinking with everyone. I slowly reached "perfection," or *drunk*, by putting down my patented pitcher of beer and lifting an entire vat of jungle juice to my face. It was tasty and delicious, and the ladies couldn't get enough of big Mitch. I even got a kiss after pounding, and then got slapped when I grabbed some chick's boobs *(She f#@king loved it.)*

After a good hour of being passed out and having hardware store industrial strength permanent marker drawings applied to his arms, chest and stomach in addition to my magnificent mask... Erick awoke.

I couldn't believe it, but the son of a bitch actually started drinking again. He drank about two beers and then disappeared for a while. Fresno State students applauded Erick on his determination to get hammered and our ability to make anything interesting. Then in a moment of complete f#@king insanity, we all saw Erick out on the ledge of the two-story complex.

By the time two of us got out there... he was sitting on the top of the hand railing, and then while standing up, he passed out, and then slid down the railing of the stairs. His unconscious body only stayed upright for seconds, but long enough to gain some momentum. He teetered backwards off the hand railing, putting his legs straight up into the air. His back smashed the foundation, flopping his head, arms, and legs backwards like a rag doll. After the smack, his body did a back flip while continually moving forward and then slammed his unshielded face into the barbecue that was cemented into the ground at the bottom of the stairs.

I thought Erick was dead. Girls screamed in horror. Yet, like Jason in a f#@king *Friday The 13th* horror movie he just kept getting up. To astonished faces, and almost-crying girls, he walked back up the stairs, tripping three times, and then lifted his shirt to see his new scar. He walked inside, muttered something completely incoherent, and then passed out for the final time.

At 4:00 in the morning our nineteen-hour straight drinking binge ended... we all slept for a good ten hours, waking up at around 2:00 in the afternoon the next day. Me with jungle juice stains all over my shirt, Erick battered and destroyed, and girls in *three different beds* with my buddies. Erick, myself, and other pals received compliments, admiration, and high-fives from all of the Fresno State people we encountered.

Throughout the night beer was pounded, girls were pounded, and the cops never came... even once. Even with the ghastly screams at 3:30 a.m. from horrified girls, or the yelling as Erick pounded two king's cups... In the end Fresno State was one hell of a time. With an abundance of females, lack of cops, cool-ass people, and cheap-ass beer, I give Fresno State a rating of six and a half keg-stands out of ten, and a college party ranking of number 8.

The final E-Dog Vomit count... 23

UNIVERSITY OF TEXAS AUSTIN

#15

When looking into UT Austin you get a lot of information about how big the campus is. I also found out they offer over 300 degree programs, and their programs are nationally ranked, blah blah... yada, yada, yada. The school's bigger because everything's bigger in Texas. I saw a hamburger bigger than my head. But if that whole "academic" thing is what you want out of college, apparently this is a decent place to go. I, on the other hand, would like the beers to be bigger and the margaritas to be bigger.

On my trip to the land of bigger crap I brought some pals with me. I needed a designated driver, and they wanted to see boobs. It was a perfect arrangement. So we began our twenty-hour drive from southern California to Austin with the hope of boobies and alcohol. I personally lost control of my hunger for vodka, and began convincing my driver that it was legal to have open alcohol containers in Arizona and New Mexico. After persuading him with lies, me and my buddy Kevin went to town on a bottle of store brand vodka.

After a good hour of slamming vodka and discussing what each of us would do for a million dollars, our driver (sober) admitted he would take a load in the mouth for a million dollars. I was very disappointed, and my buddy, Kevin, was also. To the point

of stretching his legs around the driver's seat and kicking him repeatedly... in the head... going 80 miles an hour on the freeway.

I thought it was damn funny, until I realized our driver couldn't even see the road and we drifted into the opposite lane. So I punched Kevin in the balls and instantaneously we were safe again. Thus leading me to believe that if I ever feel scared and fearful for my life, I will punch Kevin in the balls.

We arrived in Texas at 5:00 a.m. because somebody f#@ked up the timing. I blame everyone but me. Sober-boy driver suggested we check out the sights of Texas... I suggested he cup my balls with his mouth. After figuring it out, we all just passed out in the car until late afternoon. In essence, we figured everything out for nothing.

When we woke up it was around 1:00 in the afternoon and pretty damn hot. Yet in the heat of the world, women wear less clothing, so I immediately felt better. Now because of the vodka hangover, and extreme discomfort of sleeping with two guys in a car, I needed some comfort food. So I looked to score some grub, free if possible, cheap if necessary. Awesomely enough, there was a big ol' group of people in the park having a barbecue. So I told my pals to grow some testicles and follow me.

I walked up and made friends "wedding crashers" style and moved straight for the food, and how hillbilly redneck is this... They were cooking the meat in a rusty old barrel. As dirty as this is, the meat was so good I'm pretty sure I pooped a little.

Time passed pretty slowly and I was getting the alcohol itch again around 5:00 p.m. Kevin, who was very close to my level of alcoholism agreed that 5:00 p.m. had to mean happy hour somewhere. But before I could even think of where to go some older guy came up to us and asked if we paid for the food. I replied yes, as did my buddies. He then asked to see our tickets. The thought, "Aw, sh*t" ran through my head, until Kevin smashed his plate of potato salad and ribs into the guy's face and ran off. Then the thought, "Aw, f#@k" ran through my head. I stood motionless as if a T-Rex was staring right at me, but the old guy sprinted after Kevin. Then me and the driver, Paul, slowly walked in the opposite direction still continuing to eat our food.

Unbelievably we made it safely out of the park, and with a full belly. Kevin, on the other hand, called us on his cell phone 10 minutes later. The first thing out of my mouth was asking him if he didn't like the potato salad or something. He replied with a simple, "F#@k you," then told us he was in someone's back yard and he sliced his leg on a fence when he jumped over. We got the street name and off to the convenience store we went for directions.

At the store I got some directions to Kevin's hideout and I picked up some duct tape and rubbing alcohol for the wound, because we weren't sitting in the hospital all night for him. He whined for a few minutes and then realized duct tape works.

After picking up Kevin we were finally getting a chance to experience all the bars and parties Austin had to offer. Apparently Kevin's hiding spot put us right by an entire street of bars and drinking. I asked someone what this marvelous place was called, and I received an anticlimactic answer, "6th Street." We made our way in and out of bars seeing where stuff was kicking off. Eventually we ran into a place that *The Real World: Austin* cast would party at almost every weekend. I've seen the people on that show, and they get destroyed. So I figured this would be the base of operations.

During a pitcher of the sweet beer love, Kevin offered some chicks a pint. Three of the ladies came over and we poured it up. We started talking about the best spots for partying and drinking around Austin and they said we were already there. So I drank to that. She then said if the house party stuff is more your scene the fraternities are just off the west campus. So I drank to that. She then scratched her face. So I drank to that.

After a couple pitchers the ladies, who had the southern hospitality working, said we should try some other places since we were visitors. I told them we had sober Paul to drive us somewhere. Then for some reason, all three of them basically started dry humping Paul. I told him to get us over to the fraternities, and leave some for us. We got over to the Frat row around midnight, and as soon as we turned the corner it was all-out insanity.

There were people all over the place drinking and doing the best in drunken crap. I saw some tricycle races, gold fish shots, and beer box jousting. It was a kind of beautiful I can't explain. So I told Paul to get us a parking spot and we all hopped out, but son of a bitch— only minutes after getting out all three chicks spot some douche bag pretty boy and pull an N*Sync scream fest, and then ditch us. Beer money down the sh*tter. Even without the women, everyone was cool letting us in anywhere. I thought we were screwed without supplying some ladies, but everyone just wanted to get trashed and a have a good time. Every time I turned around somebody was making me pound a beer with them. Yes... Making me.

I got completely destroyed and lost track of Kevin and Paul. And that's the last I remember. One minute I was pounding a beer, and the next I was waking up on a couch in some house. No idea how I got there, no idea where I was, and Kevin and Paul were nowhere to be found.

When I woke up some dude was playing video games and saw me wake up. Right away he said, "Dude you're the f#@king man." I then wondered what the hell I did to deserve this respect. He then explained that after pounding six beers, pretty much in succession, I took a beer bong full of jungle juice. I cringed, sat up and shook the guy's hand. I then walked outside to the front lawn where there were empty pizza boxes, empty kegs, a bra, shattered pottery, and three bongs.

It was one hell of a party. With no recollection of my night or where Paul and Kevin were, I called them up. Paul made it back to the car with some girl, and Kevin was at some girl's house. Apparently Kevin got laid, Paul got laid in his car, and I did a beer bong full of jungle juice. Paul and Kevin can kiss my ass, but eventually we all got back to the car and slept until that night.

After all was said and done, I give UTA an 8 out of 10 keg stands for good booze prices, all around good times with the drinkers and easy access. And only because both my friends got laid, Ill give a 3 out of 5 pairs of boobs. If it was up to me, 0 pairs of boobs, 'cause the chicks I experienced were dumbasses who treated some hick frat boy like Justin Timberlake and mooched off our beer money. But I have to be fair; my pals got some, and maybe if I wasn't blacked out I could have pulled in something too. This school rolls in at number 15.

SAN DIEGO STATE

#7

Beautiful San Diego State, the second best party school in California. Of course, the school's take would be a little different. When you read up about San Diego State you hear a lot about the beautiful community, well rounded academics, and friendly faculty. When you take a look at a map, you realize you're less than two hours from a donkey show… or "Mexico," as some people refer to it. You're also close to the beach and surrounded by ridiculously hot women. Like, "hey she looked at me so I just jizzed myself" hot. You'll find that damn near everyone but a dumbass freshman and a poor-bastard senior trying to graduate have Friday out of school, so the weekend starts on Thursday for San Diego State.

Another big thing to note about San Diego State is the hardcore partying on holidays. St. Patty's Day, Labor Day, Fourth of July, or Halloween get some of the damn city shut down because the parties get so big. I have yet to experience the madness in San Diego on the holidays, but one day I shall.

On my trip down there I arrived around 6:00 at night, just in time for Beer Pong. I have an extensive career in the game, much more than other drinking games, and I am sometimes not allowed to play because of my greatness. So my excitement to play

was comparable to that of a little schoolgirl on her first day of class.

After arriving and going undefeated for five games, I felt like a million bucks. Yet, because I win I don't drink enough. Therefore I slammed down a good five-shotter of the Russian vodka deliciousness. Once some pre-partying was done people started throwing out names of clubs to go to like, On Broadway, Top of the Hyatt, and some other places. I quickly made it clear I'm not the club-going type and I'm much too un-pretty to hit up these places. So they started going over some bars and frats. Once someone said "PB's Bar and Grill," everyone's face lit up. So off we went, and apparently like some other bars I've been to, this one was in the good ol' MTV's *Real World*.

We arrived and the place had a pretty cool set up, palm trees outside, and surfboards strapped up on cars. It was pretty kick back and relaxing. Then 10:00 p.m. rolled around and there was a gigantic surge of people that made the place crazy. Bleach blonde girls were EVERYWHERE! At one point a friend of mine, who was destroyed, said he was so happy he wanted to do a back flip. So he went outside, flipped off his sandals and pretty much landed right on top of his head.

I thought he broke his neck, but nope, he popped right back up and said he'd try again... some other time. Spectators looked at him, ladies looked at him, and I couldn't believe it, but 15 minutes later, he actually started making out with some girl that saw him do it. I love this place! We all went back inside and took a Jaeger shot for my buddy's failed attempt.

After PB's we made it over to the Gas Lamp, which was a pretty cool spot too. A live band was playing and the people were all slaughtered, it was good times. Yet with a live band you can't really mingle with the locals, so I suggested we head back to the pad and try and get some people over. It was around 1:00 in the morning, but people were still up for it. So we went back to the pad.

When we got there, about five cars followed up the entire way, and three of them were lady's cars... God Bless America. On the way in everyone was forced to give the house's high five poster some love. I personally loved it, and high-fived it 27 times. After we got inside the drinking games

commenced. Some people did a little beer boxing, others did Kings Cup. I felt like having a little more fun on the way to getting trashed so I went with the Kings Cup. After a good hour of distractions, girls making out, and all-out drunken greatness, the final card was pulled and I slammed the deliciousness down. I got the cheers and love of the fans and then with that last blast of alcohol, the penis began doing all of my thinking.

I went off into the sea of women first in complete stupidity, and asked some girl if she'd like to see my wiener. She gave me a firm and sassy "no" and I moved on, because if at first you don't succeed, aim sluttier. So I went up to the girl doing a shot out of another girl's boobs, and I quickly asked for "my turn." They both gave me a bitchy look and walked away… F#@king lesbians. I was hitting dead ends everywhere. Mr. Lovejoy (my penis, first name Steve) was about to put himself into an inanimate object / animal if necessary. But this was not necessary because a "larger" girl was present.

I'm not proud of what I have done in some parties, and this was one of those times. Yet when all the blood has left the brain and entered Mr. Lovejoy, I have no control and deal with the consequences like a man. My consequences, in this case, were an all-out ass ripping for hours the following morning, and it didn't help there was a trail of Cheetos leading to the room I was in. My favorite slam was "Hey Mitch, you got rejected so many times you laid down a trail of Cheetos to reel in the big one, eh?" Son of a bitch.

After the ass ripping was completed, or at least settled down, I had to give San Diego State a 7 out of 10 keg stands because the booze was a little pricey, but people were down to use every last cent to get trashed. And 5 out of 5 pairs of boobs because the women here were damn near ALL playboy status, except my love pillow. They were also pretty cool except when you tried to make drunken advances on them.

SUNY NEW PALTZ

#12

Its not every day I end up on the East Coast, but I finally made it to New York. When I looked into schools in New York lots of them publicized their acting schools, business majors, and beyond the academic it was all about the outdoors. Camping, hiking, rock climbing, etc. For a guy with the stereotypical view that New York is one gigantic city, I was surprised to find out there was a lot of wilderness to New Paltz. But as many have come to know, I could care less about nature-y tree hugging crap like that. And I met some of the "business majors" and some of them were getting more f#@ked up than me! Hopefully some pictures of them can be used as blackmail later on in life when I've drinken? drunken? dranked myself into homelessness and alcoholism.

I got a hold of my pal Gary who attended New Paltz and he said it was a helluva party spot, and there was a lot to do. Because nothing else in New York was really putting a tickle in my pickle I went for it. I never really heard of the place but, when I got off the plane and back to his pad I could smell the vagina, and second hand marijuana all over the place. It was

glorious. Then when I walked to the fridge I saw one of the most beautiful things ever.... A refrigerator so loaded with beer, that they actually put one in the egg compartment.

I was tempted to kiss Gary, but I held it back for I am not a homosexual. I just cracked open a beer, patted his ass and told him "Good Game," which was completely un-homosexual. Gary wasn't part of a fraternity, but he knew a lot of guys in the Greek world, so this was my in. He said the bars were pretty awesome too, but dirty as all hell. He said a place called P and G's was a great place to kick-start the night. I explained that I was going nowhere until his fridge was empty. We compromised and I pounded three beers, did two in a beer bong in ten minutes, put six more beers in my coat, and then continued on our way to P and G's.

This place was awesome; I can't believe all the cool-ass people that were in there. Some chick actually bought *ME* a beer. When the hell does that happen?! It was one of those bar / restaurant places which usually turns me off, but dammit this place raped all other bar / restaurants I've been to… yes, raped. I probably spent 200 dollars in an hour and a half, even with six beers in my coat. I couldn't help it, everyone was happy and plastered and cool as hell. The chicks were hardcore though. One of them even wanted to arm-wrestle me. Out of fear of losing to a girl, I merely laughed at her and then pretended I was in the middle of a conversation elsewhere.

Eventually Gary told me karaoke was about to start up. I'm not too big on the singing, but with so much beer in me it sounded like the best thing to do… EVER. So I put on "Free Falling" by Tom Petty and rocked that sh*t out. I also chose it because no other song gets an assload of drunks to start singing along better than "Free Falling." I think the entire bar got in on it. I made myself a lot of friends over there on the East Coast, and you would be surprised how many chicks get turned on just by me saying I'm from California. It was the easiest

time I've ever had to make out with women. Gary kept track and he said that I made out with nine girls at that bar, and triple kissed another set. Although I didn't knock a load out, I was still impressed with myself. So impressed that I bought myself an "Adios motherf#@ker," which made me black out.

Blacking out sucks balls, especially when my pal Gary can pretty much make up anything he wants, and I pretty much have to believe him. Like "Yeah dude, you started making out with a transvestite," or "Yeah dude, you threw up on the bar and then licked it back up." I never received confirmation that this happened, so I call bullsh*t.

Although I blacked out for a few hours, I still have the memory of walking to some chick's car afterwards. Me and Gary both had chicks with us and it was an interesting walk to the car. Boob grabbing, wiener grabbing, ass rubbing, tongue fighting, we found some real champion ladies. The car ride home was fun too, apparently DUI's aren't anything to worry about in New Paltz. When we made it back to Gary's the drunk munchies hit me full force. I was too lazy to cook the meat in the fridge, and too hungry not to start drinking the bottles of barbecue sauce.

Half way into the bottle of barbecue sauce, everything starts coming back up. Panic sets in, but I still have my wits about me, and in order to avoid losing my lady of the evening I ran outside. Now here's the best part, one of my asshole crowing achievements. Gary tells the girls to make themselves at home, and then follows me outside. Instead of making it to a bush, I laid down a new barbecue sauce-colored paint job on the girl's driver side window.

In my defense, I did not purposefully do this. I merely lost my balance, caught one arm on the top of the car and lost control. Anyone who has drunken-yacked knows that once the yacking starts you're pretty much paralyzed. So there was nothing I could do to avoid the car. After my double taste of barbecue sauce, I rinsed my mouth out with beer and then proceeded to hookup, with the chick whose car I just vomited on. If you've stopped reading at this point and began applauding, I appreciate your respect. Or, if you're an uptight assface who can't laugh at the misfortune of others, you shouldn't be reading my material.

After it was all said and done, the hangover did the night justice. It was one of the top five hangovers of all time for me. When you spend 250 dollars at a bar, sing Tom Petty with 300 drunk people, vomit on a girls car, then wake up next to her hung over as hell I call that a damn good night. So New Paltz, I give you an 8 out of 10 keg stands and 4 out of 5 pairs of boobs. Decent alcohol prices, good availability of booze, and nice looking women who like to make out and put out. YEE HAW!! SUNY New Paltz rolls in at number 12.

UNIVERSITY OF CALIFORNIA SANTA BARBARA

#1

Before getting into what the school has to say about the campus, I'll have to admit that UC Santa Barbara is probably one of the sexiest f#@king locations I have ever been to. A huge beach community with the smell of ocean everywhere, and perfect 72-degree weather damn near year round. I'm going to retire here… or die here… whichever comes first. I put my money on death.

…Palm-framed vistas of the blue Pacific and the golden Santa Ynez Mountains. The scent of eucalyptus mixed with the saltwater breeze. Here on the edge of the Pacific, many of the country's most promising students join a community of scholars whose accomplishments are internationally recognized and whose skills as teachers of undergraduates are evident each day in classrooms and laboratories. In the humanities and the arts as well as in engineering and the sciences, UC Santa Barbara introduces students to novel ways of thinking, learning, and conducting research…

I've gotta hand it to the school, they gave a pretty good description of the place. It's damn fine looking, and students here really do have novel ways of thinking, learning and conducting research. This was the first place that I saw five guys drink an entire keg by themselves in order to count exactly how many cups were inside. Not sure what for, but I salute the scientific efforts they put forth to count up the ounces. This was also the first time I actually saw a bong made out of a pear. I guess an upper class glass-blown bong just isn't in the budget when you have to pay almost 1,300 dollars for a one-bedroom apartment.

When you visit the mighty college of Santa Barbara the first thing almost anyone sees is the unbelievable amount of attractive women… and if during the day, totally bikini'd out. It's f#@king ridiculous. I had a boner all day, and most the night until I got too drunk to have one anymore. After we got there we went to check things out. It's only a small walk to the beach where sh*t-loads of people go to drink and have day beach parties. There's coolers in the sand, yet again females in bikinis, all around f#@king awesomeness.

When the time comes to buy alcohol, like when driving into town... you have a few choices for alcoholic beverages, but no matter where you go, you get ROCK BOTTOM prices. I pay more for Tic-Tacs in Santa Barbara than beer. There was a keg of Milwaukee's Best for 34 dollars... 34 F#@KING DOLLARS!! FOR A KEG?! I pissed myself. I then noticed something even more amazing... an 11 dollar 30-pack of natural light. So cutting out the price of keg cups, we just made out even better, as fellow alcoholic Wes Lange shows you here.

Even when the going is tough, and there is no beer bong in sight, it takes the ingenuity of a man like my buddy Wes to slice off the bottom of a water bottle and then have good-looking women pour beer into his mouth. It's this kind of amazing problem solving ability that makes Santa Barbara so academically profound.

Six years ago Chico State was still the king of Halloween. Then following Halloween 2001's night of multiple stabbings, rapes, MIP's, DUI'S, and thefts, the entire city board ass-raped all of Halloween. The next year SWAT vans were everywhere, helicopters, riot police on every street, they took away Port-o-Potties, and enforced "zero tolerance." They can zero tolerance my dick. So a few people got stabbed... no one died right? It's all in good fun. So basically I couldn't scratch my balls without getting a ticket. This forced another school to come up – and Santa Barbara did.

Entire three-mile long streets were FILLED with people. There was alcohol everywhere; slutty, tightly dressed women were even more slutty and tightly dressed. "DP," or Del Playa Road, had a party at every house stretching for five miles and you

could barely move with the insane amount of people. But it is a lot easier to take a piss when the cops can't even fit in to give tickets for urinating in public. Women were everywhere. Insanity was all over. Fights, nudity, alcohol, the beach, all in all, Santa Barbara is the new college king of Halloween.

On a Tuesday night in college, most people would expect rest, studying, TV watching, etc. Yet in Santa Barbara... there's a heavy flow of beer, and Jell-O wrestling matches. If that doesn't make you happy about life, you should kill yourself now. How F#@KING AWESOME is that?! – Hot chicks volunteering to "wrestle" each other in Jell-O for the amusement of a party crowd. Some people have sunsets, some people have Picasso, some even have bestiality videos. I have Tuesday night in Santa Barbara.

From the students and residents in Santa Barbara you get lots of people blabbering on and on about the actual rate of STDs in the area. "50 percent of the students have something," "Dude, I know 10 people that go there and 9 of 'em have open sores on their garbage or face." I've heard a lot from people at the school or who know someone from there. The statistic is actually around 1 in 3 students tested by the school's student health center have contracted a STD. So it's not necessarily an accurate number, because only 10 to 15 percent of the students have been tested at their wellness center. So it's perfectly ok to go out and get some sweet lovin'.

Right?... Oh Jesus, I think I can feel the syphilis...

With all out insanity almost any night of the week, beautiful women everywhere, the cops who are almost cooler than some college kids, a beach for something to do only a minute away, beer prices low as all hell and a high probability of getting some ass... You just can't beat this place; Santa Barbara makes it easy to call them number 1. 10 out of 10 keg stands and 5 out of 5 pairs of boobs, this place f#@k starts your FACE!

A WORD

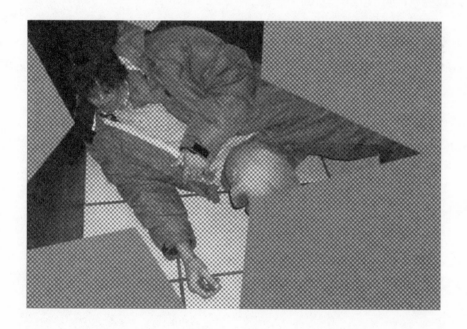

Brock Spady - YouTube Star

When Van came to me and asked me to take part in the *Van Wilder Guide To Graduating College In Eight Years Or More*, two things came to mind: 1.) I thought I had blocked his number. And 2.) What was it I had to say about college that he couldn't say himself? He survived nearly 16 semesters of college life, while I only experienced an embarrassingly low 4 years of university, and foolishly graduated on time. That, he said, was precisely his point.

While visiting me at Mason, he noted the diverse campus and ever-changing student body. He said he has come to realize, "that whole time stops for no one thing" and it was really starting to depress him. After bonging a few Natty Lites and hooking up with a freshman in my bathroom, he seemed to be feeling better.

We walked the campus at dusk and discussed the path we saw college heading down. He was upset with the changes he saw students making. Thanks to T9, guys nowadays are so text-savvy, their oral communication skills are being confined to drunken cunnilingus. Girls used to want to look smart and sophisticated; now they just want to look easy. What happen to all the quick-witted smartass guys and unattainable beautifully brained girls? On the rare happenstance that you do witness some original wit, the speaker is so equally surprised he laughs at himself louder than his audience. The only place you can still find the smart and beautiful woman is in-between the dinosaur and the dodo on nature's extinction list. I told him change was inevitable; it's a part of life.

"I've taken Biology four times, Brock. I know this isn't the direction humans should be evolving," he said. "They need more help than one man can provide."

With that in mind, Van asked me to contribute anything and everything that might help a new student skip a few steps. These steps are not to be omitted in hopes of graduating earlier, but in an effort to bypass all of the bull and get straight to the good stuff. This is for all the students who don't want to have to sit at every lunch table just to find out they're considered a meathead and should be sitting in the jock section. This is for all the students that want to leave school with more than a couple of cool stories to tell their friends once they move back in with their parents. You need to have your facts straight if you want to have any sort of control over this untamed beast they call school.

So what did he mean by advice? Advice is something good friends give each other based on their own experiences. I'm stubborn and didn't heed Van's advice when he told me to stay in school as long as possible, and I wish I had. He, on the other hand, gladly accepted my advice. He asked me how to get back to Coolidge University from my place by only taking the back roads, and I told him. My directions were dead on, and therefore I now have a spot in his book.

That's my first piece of advice. People want to help people that help them. So quit walking around campus like a Japanese tourist in Times Square. Give visitors directions, nod to people you don't know, and light that guy's cigarette. You're in the majors now (unless you're attending a community college) so start acting like it. Make an impression early, and a girl late. Make a friend everyday, and a bong everyway. Drop a class, and kick some ass. Do it all, and do it now. These are going to be the best eight or so years of your life.

10 Things You Can NEVER Let A Best Friend Do

Since the dawn of our existence, mankind has been prone to concoct inane thoughts, try impossible feats, and head down paths no soul has traveled before. While college is undoubtedly the place to approach these situations and ideas and apply the scientific method, there will always be a few we wish we had left on the drawing board. Thankfully, that's why we have best friends. Though often the inspiration behind the ideas in the first place, ultimately they should serve as the balancing force on your weighted debate over whether or not to actually cannon ball off the roof into that baby-pool filled with Jell-O. This list doesn't apply to females and their unexplainably shady relationships with one another. These things are MAN-datory for a reason.

No.1 Fight Solo
Yep, he got you into it, and it's up to you to get the two of you out of it. Having a best friend is like always having someone in your corner. Remember, no matter how wrong he is, just like Hillary, you stick by your man.

No. 2 Drink Your Last Beer
Now what kind of friend would he be if you let him do this? Let him do this today, and tomorrow he'll be asking you to soap his junk in the shower. Whoever drinks the last beer, buys more. Period.

No. 3 Let His Girlfriend Move In

No, no, no. First she'll be really nice to you. Then she'll start cleaning. Then she'll start giving him just enough sex to melt his manhood and memory, leaving a hollow shell that's become a mere shadow for your new female flat mate.

No. 4 Go to Jail Alone

You really want your BFF to cry himself to sleep in someone else's lap? (NOTE: If the charge is murder or worse, better let him ride this horse alone. That doesn't mean you're off the hook; you must be at the courthouse the next morning to bail him out.)

No. 5 Wear That

Most guys could care less about what they're wearing, and that's the way it should be; but there are a few things that just shouldn't be done. What right do you have to tell him you can't pop that collar and wear socks with those flip-flops? Every right, my friend, you have every right in the world.

No. 6 F#@k Your Sister

Come on, man. That's just wrong.

No. 7 Drink By Himself

So his girlfriend leaves him for his physics professor the night before your big final. He's going to drink his angst away while you study weaknesses in the economic structure of a small-businesses' import market? I think not. You can reevaluate your test materials by examining how his steady intake of domestics lowers his interest in foreign affairs, increases his compatibility, and opens his market for possibilities.

No. 8 Date Your Old Girlfriend

He should trust your judgment on this one and just stay away. Your friendship will always outlast their relationship, and when it's all over he'll be the one feeling like sh*t. Save him the pain.

Asking things like, "How do I taste?" and "Does she still only swallow?" should speed up the process.

VanWilderism #78
Superficiality is only skin-deep.
Write that down.

No. 9 Get the Best of You

If he can never get the best of you, then obviously he can't let you get the best of him. Does this create a never-ending string of insults, slaps, challenges, dares, and contest? Yes, yes it does. They call it friendship.

No. 10 Cock Block

I'm sure you're wondering why "Screw a fat chick" wasn't on here. Well, that's because real friends don't cock block. Have faith that your compadré can get rid of that unwanted tail if he desires. A few exceptions here: if you know she's infested with a ball-flesh eating bacteria, or you think she is a he, you're allowed to step in and protect him and his two "best-friends."

10 Things You MUST Have
On You At All Times

Don't leave home without 'em. These are those absolutely necessary items you must have on your body to survive any college situation. If you've never needed an item on this list, you will. Heed its advice and plan ahead. You won't be sorry.

No. 1 Condoms
It's pretty much self-explanatory. Sex happens. Be ready.

No. 2 Rolling Papers
What's worse than not having any green? Having green, and nothing to smoke it with. If I had a nickel for every time a half-naked babe has put away her stash because my wallet didn't hold the rolling papers I promised... I'd have a nickel. Because that sh*t only has to happen once. Trust me.

No. 3 Cell Phone
I once went two and a half weeks without my cell phone to prove to a friend it was possible. I also read about a man going three weeks without food or water. I wouldn't suggest either.

No. 4 Lighter
Nothing feels more helpless than being a man in the twenty-first century who is unable to produce fire. Even if you don't smoke, do you really have the heart to tell her you can't light her fire?

No. 5 An ID That Can Get You Drinks

So your face is smoother than a cue ball and your voice cracks more often than Rosie O's wicker rocking chair. Your ID makes it clear you're 32 and just shaved before walking out the door.

No. 6 Sharpie

There's no telling when some bathroom wall or a sleeping drunkard's face will require your artistic signature. Your paintbrush should always be within reach.

No. 7 Underwear

The day you forget it will be the day no one forgets you. If you don't want others to see you naked, odds are they don't want to either. Take my word on this one; if you go to a toga party, you'll leave without a toga. You want to keep your undies clean and unseen.

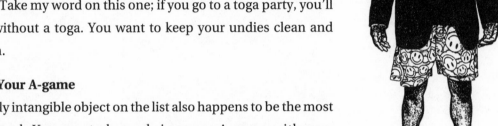

No. 8 Your A-game

The only intangible object on the list also happens to be the most misplaced. You must always bring your A-game with you, everywhere you go. This can be difficult for some people because they only come equipped with an unflattering "C-game."

No. 9 Gum

No, not because your breath stinks, because hers does. I can't even count the times I've had to skip foreplay because I couldn't stand to make out with some rotten-mouthed Jane Blow. Treat yourself to a piece then casually offer your partner some. If she doesn't take the hint, follow with an earnest "please."

No. 10 Running Feet

Regardless of what shoes you're wearing, your running feet should be on underneath. No matter how chill a party looks or how relaxed your mind is, your feet should be ready to bolt. Anytime you hear the word "Cops!" your subconscious will take over, and

VanWilderism #229
Being in deep sh*t is just as
bad as shallow sh*t.
Write that down.

you will often experience a temporary blackout. If this occurs, stay calm. You'll awake mid-run two blocks away wondering how you got there. Just thank your running feet, finish your beer, and walk the rest of the way home.

10 Things You Must Do Before Leaving College

College would have been synonymous with "The Land of Opportunity" had not that pesky Arkansas already claimed it. With or without the nickname, the possibilities are boundless here. Saying there are only ten things to do before you graduate is ridiculous, but so is creating a list of the thousands of different paths you can take. Here are the ten most basic claims to fame that should be on your wall keeping your diploma company.

No. 1 Sex It Up

This could have a top ten in itself. Two girls at once, flip-flaps, flap-jacks, and nap-taps. Waffle towers, apple sours, Roman flowers and happy hours. BJs, HJs, RJs, and XYZJs. Do it all. This is the time in your life you'll never stop regretting if you don't take advantage of it now. So go ahead, be a freak on her, take a leak on her, whatever floats your boat and sinks your ship. It's all good.

No. 2 Get Drunk

This seems like a no-brainer, right? When I say get drunk, I mean it. Start drinking before breakfast and have that case finished by noon. Drink Sunday to Sunday one week. Have nothing but margaritas the next. Test your limits and build up endurance now, because after college they won't call you a student anymore. They prefer the term, alcoholic.

No. 3 You're Banned!

Find a bar you like, become a regular, then piss them the hell off. Destroying the bathroom and starting fights have always worked for me. Once banned, make sure to try and frequent the establishment at least once every few months to keep them on their toes. Nothing tells your friends or date you're a badass like, "Hey, I thought we told you never to show your face in here again!"

No. 4 Just Say "Yes" To Drugs

Drugs are bad, mmkay. We all know that. But do you know why? Hit that doobie, rip that bong, and chew those mushrooms good. This is the one time when being high for no reason is not only acceptable, but also understandable because your professor can't fire you and your RA can't evict you. Just keep it to yourself when that LSD starts turning your classroom tile floor into a mosaic representation of your life's journey. Warning: Crack is whack and don't ever do anything that comes in a syringe. Fo' real.

No. 5 I Don't Feel Tardy

Sure, class is loads of fun, but there are some days when sitting on your ass appears much more beneficial to your foreseeable future. You have to skip class for no reason whatsoever at least once a semester. This doesn't count if you spend the time running errands or catching up on missed work. We call those workdays.

No. 6 Spring Breaktacula

Unless the rock you've been living under doesn't get basic cable, you're more than well aware of what Spring Break entails. Like Vegas, what happens on Spring Break stays on Spring Break. Bring your camera for sightseeing, but leave it at the hotel once it's time to party. Your future children will thank you for this one.

No. 7 Fight Night, Round 3:00 a.m.

You've been drinking all night and someone just spilt their drink on you when you stumbled into them. His mistake. Punch this asshole in the nose. Getting into fights is a part of growing up. You need to be in some now, so you'll know not to next time.

No. 8 Road Tripping

Campus is great, but those dorm walls grow closer every night. Grab two or three friends and hit the open road. Grab tickets to a concert out of state, or pack up your old camping gear and have a guys' night out. When it's all over, these are the events you'll remember. Everything else will be one big party.

No. 9 Rush Da' Floor

Whether or not you're a sports fanatic shouldn't matter when it comes to representing the home team. Follow your team all the way. Make sure to be at every home game you can. When your home team underdogs stomp the visiting State A-holes, be sure you're one of the first to hit the hardwood. The mob mentality is overwhelming and unforgettable. Finding your head on SportsCenter that night will be the icing on the cake. You'll have one of those cool "I was there" stories to bore your grandchildren to sleep with.

No. 10 Get a Job

Yes, you must get a job before graduating college. You'd be surprised how many kids can go 22 years off a hefty allowance. Getting your first job during college is similar to getting your first pubic hair during puberty. You're not sure of its purpose yet, but you do feel a strange sense of pride and maturity for having acquired one. Not only will you feel older, but you'll be able to buy at least one fancy 6-pack of dank beer for every three cases of watered down crap you normally afford.

VanWilderism #82
You can't find "Someday" on the calendar.
Write that down.

Too Cliché

As clichéd as it might seem, you'll find that college actually is composed of all those little stereotypical cliques movies and high school have been smothering us with. Navigating your way through these contrived masses is critical to control the timing and placement of your social status in the public college life. Freshmen often tend to attach themselves to the first people they meet since they're in this "new and scary" place. These first friends can end up being your best friend or your biggest mistake. This guide should help you determine what to look for, what to stay away from, and some dead giveaways.

Jocks

Jocks are the only mentally handicapped students allowed in Honors Classes and could give a rat's ass. They'll often be the first to tell you how they *"didn't done alls that well and school but no oned cared 'cause they Went ALL THE WAY! Ugh-yeah!"* Many believe their lowered intelligence is what allows them to be the only group in the animal kingdom consisting of all alpha males. Thinking that their performance on the field and physique should be enough to get laid, they're equipped with horrendous male-to-female communication skills. They take *every* game very, very seriously. They often find little obscure sports facts and repeat them constantly to feel as if they're educating. Not knowing a reference to one of their facts might label you a "conflict" in their book. Fears include nudity and politics.

DEAD GIVEAWAYS:

The Fitted Cap:

They just don't leave home without it. Can be worn either casually forward askew to the right or left, or backward with the fitted strap covering the eyebrows.

The Armless Armoire:

They go sleeveless to the gym, sleeveless to class, sleeveless to the clubs, sleeveless to the funerals. Their biceps are often in perma-flex.

This Article:

In reading this article if they agreed to this classification until they came across "fear of nudity" and adamantly refuted it. Possibly offering to expose themselves on the spot as proof.

Dudes

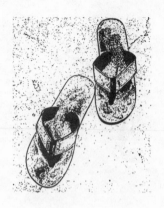

These guys are often considered the most "chill" people on campus. Their lax and easy-going lifestyle leads them to dabble in a wide variety of activities but not necessarily become proficient in any of them. They avoid conflict by laughing and breaking eye contact. They call almost everyone, dude. They call everyone else, man. Odds are they won't know how long to defrost your 20-lb Thanksgiving Day turkey, but they can sure cook the sh*t out of some macaroni and cheese. These half-ass Renaissance men are most likely to have some skill in: skateboarding, guitar, smoking pot, Madden, snowboarding, surfing, school work, hackey sacking, basketball, drawing, beer pong, and quoting Sublime songs.

DEAD GIVEAWAYS:

Flip-Flops In The Winter:

Rain, Sleet, Snow or Lava, the flip-flops will be on.

Styled Bedhead Haircut:

If it looks like he spent time trying to make it look like he just got out of bed…

One Skater, Straight Up, Hold the Board:

He wears only skate clothes, yet never rides a board, and still thinks trucks are made by Ford.

Emo Kids

Emo Kids see themselves as the new age punks. Their pampered bullsh*t existence has been so terribly emotional and traumatic they're ready to throw in the towel before they're twenty. They hate society almost as much as they hate their parents. Life is this big depressing drama, and if you don't agree you're a blind, preppy idiot. They only open up around their friends, and can fall in love at the drop of a hat. They think they know this secret side to life no one else sees.

DEAD GIVEAWAYS:

Ah Sir, This is the Women's Dressing Room:
Nothing feels better than a tight pair of chick pants. The extra small crotch area stitched in women's jeans can often be helpful in determining the sex of the Emo Kid in question.

Broken Record Rock:
No matter where you see them, you'll hear them listening to the same band. They will claim it's a different band, but the only evidence will be in the appearance of the CD. The audible content will be identical. Whether or not there is actually more than one Emo band has yet to be determined.

No, it's MY Space:
Despite what they'll admit, they love MySpace. It's how their band will make their big break. If not in a band, they're star struck by the local bands who they feel an intimate connection with.

Jackasses

If he starts sentences with, "Dare me to..." odds are he's a Jackass. The equation is simple: pain = hilarity, right? Always the first to break something or someone, the school Jackasses have an appetite for danger, destruction, the occasional dismemberment, and even disembowelment. Though excruciating to watch, it is considered far less painful than having to tell them "it's only funny when the guys on TV do it," and having to crush their small childlike spirits. They may seem lost and on a pointless mission, but they are out to prove something. They're making a statement. They're just not sure what that statement is yet.

DEAD GIVEAWAYS:

The Crime Scene Investigator's Dream Job:

The guys and gals over at CSI would have a field day with these human test dummies. Nine times out of ten they are carrying multiple samples of blood, urine, and semen. Often mixed together with a hair sample. Their clothes often reflect their last six weeks of activity and everything they've done has been filmed and posted online.

Stunt-Single For Hire:

Who needs a stunt double? Who needs cut-aways or multiple angles? Not me. I want it all in one shot. I talk into the camera, put the cat poo in my mouth, light my hair on fire, get punched in the face, fall back through the glass table, vomit straight up in the air, shower myself in liquid feline feces, and put out the fire in the same move. Cut camera. Haha, that's funny, right? Right? RIGHT?!

Penny Whore:

They'll do anything for a dollar. And I mean, <u>anything</u>...

Frat Boys

Can you blame, 'em? Yes. Yes, you very well can. One thing you must understand about a frat is, the brotherhood-bill. They really want to be your friend, your best friend at that, but there's that whole little thing with the brotherhood-bill. Have you paid the brotherhood-bill yet? They really, really want to be your friend and talk and hangout, you just gotta sign up and pay your dues. I mean, if you'd just join this wouldn't be a problem. Cause as soon as you pay we'll all be best friends and have no fights and bouts of jealously. We'll all just be really close and do anything for each other. If you need any of us, we'll ALL be there for you in a heartbeat. No questions asked. Except the, "have you paid your dues" question which is mandatory in any occasion.

DEAD GIVEAWAYS:

Unicorny:

Haircuts are easy. Make it all short, except this little tuft dead center of the forehead. Make that hair 2-3 times as long, mousse it, spike it, set it, and forget it! Well, at least until you walk by a mirror, bathroom, or shiny thing.

The Entourage:

They have a table in the cafeteria where the same people sit everyday. They travel in packs because they feel going to new places alone might make them look un-cool. They think showing up everywhere with fifteen people, and not introducing themselves, or meeting new people, is definitely the way to get the full college experience.

Like a Blind Kid on a Rubik's Cube:

Playing with girls sure is fun. Too bad they have no idea what they're doing. They prefer easy girls with no brains; acceptable face not required. They view their relationships as if they're the next Brad and Angelina, minus all the people that actually care.

Smokers

What's the very first thing you crave when you wake up? Eggs and Bacon? Sex? A long warm shower? Sex in the shower? No, how about we put on a hoodie and go sit outside on the cold cement and have ourselves a cigarette? Yeah, that sounds kickass. Smokers love to smoke. They smoke more than they eat, read, walk, or fart. A pack a day keeps the jitters away. Cigarettes get them a break every hour at work, and a perfect exit out of any conversation. "Man, I need a cigarette. Excuse me." Most college smokers only smoke when they drink, but real Smokers only breathe when they smoke. Most people aren't personally offended until they try to make out with said Smoker. Then all those anti-smoking commercials come rushing back, and you innocently but firmly push their head down south.

DEAD GIVEAWAYS:

Tarter, Tarter Everywhere...:
And not a spot is clean. Their canine incisors could be a paint sample for the repainting of your old ride to school.

Cigs, You Can Take 'Em Anywhere!:
You've probably seen them riding a bike while smoking a cigarette, and odds are they burn them even faster running. A true Smoker will smoke in any situation a jack can be lit.

OK, Mr. Quit, I Guess I Can Squeeze You in Sometime After March:
Oh, they're going to quit. No need to give them advice. They're just not going to quit now, when they're only a few years in. Nah, they're going to wait till after college when their addiction has grown weaker and will be crippled by their drive to succeed. Yeah, that's how they'll do it.

Token Tokers

If you are high right now, reading this, you could be a Toker. If you are high right now off someone else's weed, you could be a Token Toker. There's always one. That guy who never has any of his own. That guy who magically appears every time the bong is whipped out. That guy whose nose you would have broken a long time ago had you not been high every time you've encountered him. They talk about pot 24/7. They probably claim to be the biggest smoker in the area code and assume themselves to be the most powerful smoker in the room. Their pamphlet-like knowledge of the subject might have caused you to hate them immediately. They will never change the subject. Get rid of this douche bag. Now.

DEAD GIVEAWAYS:

My Father Was A Drug Dog:

These little leeches can smell some weed. No matter where you are, the second you break it out they're right around the corner. The marijuana does not even need to be lit for one of these bitches to catch the sent.

I'll Mow Your Grass for Free:

If you've ever made the mistake of giving them a green hit, or anything close to it, you've noticed their attention to detail. During inhale, they'll start at the edge of the green and work the lighter up and down the rows until all the colors have changed to orange and blackened out.

The Annoying Factor:

For some reason, every word that comes out of their mouth pisses you off. Everyone hates the Token Toker, yet he seems to have no clue. It amazes you how little he has to do to get your blood boiling. Again, get rid of this douche bag. Now.

Big and Bitten (the Vampire Effect)

This is the big girl who can't seem to see herself in a mirror. She thinks she looks good in sh*t Jessica Alba can't wear. She believes you find a super huge fake level of confidence "sexy." In a crowded bar, asking her to move aside in hopes of avoiding contact with her cold, clammy mid-range could start a tussle. A simple R&B ring-tone is all that is required to start an intense risqué dance session. You will either find them being a bitch, or pretending to not be a bitch.

DEAD GIVEAWAYS:

That Says What?:

Shirts with lettering that look like the newest Dali creation. Only James Lipton can stretch words further than these classy girls. Often the key word or punchline on the shirt will be covered by a towering shadow forcing you to closely examine the phrase when she catches you looking at it, much to her pleasure and your chagrin.

The Doctor Is Out:

The soles of her sandals have blown and collapsed into themselves like a dark star. The trillion pounds of pressure have changed the rubber into a new undocumented element. They say their feet are killing them, but ask yourself… Who is really doing the killing here?

Were Those My Pants You're Wearing?!:

They borrow clothes knowing you'd never really feel the same about the article after they've worn it. The tag still might say "2," but now that your friend has multiplied them by 8, your new "16s" aren't exactly your favorite jeans anymore.

Long Distance Dalliances

Aw, how cute. She has a boyfriend back home she's in love with. And of course, there's no way any one of her 5,000 new co-ed classmates could possibly be a better match for her. Watch out for these psychos. They'll use their sweetie 600-miles down the street to avoid social interactions and chances are she hates the school and everyone there. Emotionally, they will cheat their ass off, but when the two of you get alone, you'll be lucky to score a half-assed blowjob. You can bark up that tree all semester if you'd like. They're "comfortable" how they are and may never see the bigger picture.

DEAD GIVEAWAYS:

Can You Hear Me Now?:

Their cell phone acts as a baby monitor and they can dial their honey's digits faster than "911." As soon as they are out of class the phone hits their ear. They stay up till 5:00 a.m. explaining why they stopped by "this one little party for like five minutes that wasn't even that cool anyway" every night to some insecure prick boyfriend who is whimpering with anger and jealously on the other end.

Seven Degrees of My Boyfriend:

No matter what subject you're on, they'll be able to relate it to their insignificant other. After finishing another story no one cared about, they'll let a few minutes pass before interrupting with a loud laugh spurred by something the boyfriend had done eight months prior.

Agoraphobia Anyone?:

You've once seen them at a party – literally, once. And that's just because they were returning a book to the girl that lived upstairs. Sulking in solitude is always more fun than social interaction with new and exciting people. Try to take them out and you'll end up hating them by the time you actually drag them out the door.

Iuse'tas

It's too bad you met them in college, because if you like them now, you would have loved them back then. Iuse'tas used to do a lot of things. They used to be in great shape. They used to have tons of friends, romances, and adventures. Of course they used to make straight A's. Before long you'll have trouble remembering why you *used to* like them in the first place. They'll talk for hours about their old best friend and the deep timeless bond they share. Funny this friend never visits or even returns phone calls. Careful, asking them what they do now could cause them to start an hour-long narrative explaining how they fell off the beaten path. Clarifying your question won't get you any closer to an answer, so don't even try.

DEAD GIVEAWAYS:

Who's the Kid?:

Photos of a forgotten child lace their bedroom walls. The photos are from before their big weight gain or acne attack. "See how cute I was?" These photos often create a mural of old high school photographs, apparently documenting every time they smiled in the 90's.

These Pom-Poms Could Come In Handy Some Day:

Why did they bring their old cheering squad outfit with them to college? I don't know, and I'm not going to ask.

I Do All My Shopping At High School:

I don't know what school they went to, but they sure gave out a hell of a lot of free t-shirts. If every shirt they wear came from high school, or a one-time event, or a family reunion, they've got Iuse'ta written all over them.

Musically Mused

They only like bands you've never heard. They think everyone's "new sh*t" sucks. They'll bitch for hours about how screwed-up and blind the world is for not recognizing their favorite experimental garage gods, and yet if the public does catch on, then the band "sold out." You've never seen them without headphones and concerts are considered their second home. These kids can be cool if and only if you never discuss music with them, which is all they talk about. Their favorite artists are the only ones that understand them, and "you wouldn't understand their music." Try asking them about bands that don't exist. When they tell you they've never heard of them give them a disbelieving, "Really?! Huh." If they pretend they have heard of the band, confess you made it up and watch them scramble to explain how they really had heard of a band called "The Baby Sausage Oyster-Toe Experiment."

DEAD GIVEAWAYS:

Converse Amongst Yourselves :

The Chuck Taylors are essential. They will have a pair of these shoes, guaranteed. Most likely customized by years of toe tapping, nervous picking and random doodling. Sometimes they even acknowledge others bearing their same taste with a "members only" style wave, much like motorcyclists and Jeep owners.

Check Out the Concert Chronology on Carmen:

They don't just remember every band they've ever heard of, they remember when they heard them for the first time. "Oh yeah, I liked them back in March of '87. Back before that single of theirs came out." The fact that they were in the first grade then doesn't matter. "My older sister was really into them, so I heard all this stuff back then." Don't bother arguing.

The Stub Hub:

They have more ticket stubs than, …well. They have a lot.

Really Sporty Spices

Really Sporty Spices are always on the move. They walk fast, their hair is always up, and the only type of "make-up" they have any experience with are the mandatory make-up games they have after a home game is rained out. These chicks think they're the hardest bitches on the planet, and they probably are. Odds are they'll wipe the floor with you in a pick-up game, but you'd beat them in a beauty pageant any day, despite your sex. They try to be "one of the guys" but it never works, and never will. When they have to clean up for a dance or something formal, everyone tells them how pretty they are, but that's only in comparison to what they normally look like. Trying to slide a dress off their squared shoulders is like pulling a turtleneck sweater off a hanger, through the neck.

DEAD GIVEAWAYS:

Spontaneous Calisthenics:

They wear sweat pants to practice, sweats to class, sweats to church, sweats to the Lilith Fair. They give off a look of "I'm going to bust out into something physically challenging any second now." There's no doubt their bodies are in great shape, but their lesbian volleyball coach is the only one who gets any pleasure out of it. All we get are the sweatpants. And they only look hot on sorority girls.

Hey Dude, You're Cute:

They call members of the opposite sex "dude" or "man" as a way of showing they like you, but see you as only a friend. If she calls you "buddy" I assure you it won't become the "bosom" kind.

With Karate They'll Kick Your Ass:

Really Sporty Spices throw more punches than de la Hoya. Their goal is to punch you as hard as they can, because they know you have to pretend like it doesn't hurt. And it wouldn't, if their fist were bigger than the tip of a pickaxe.

Camera Queens

Camera Queens have more pictures of themselves online than Jessica Simpson. They are the only person who would ever bring a camera to a grocery store. "Here's Jessica, buying beer! 2 Cute!" They're always tagging you in pictures you don't remember being taken and leaving inside joke comments you don't even get. None of the pictures are candid. Mostly posed shots where it's obvious those being photographed were having their patience tested. All photos are "good ones" unless it's a picture of them; then it's "Oh, I look stupid in this one." No, that's how you always look.

DEAD GIVEAWAYS:

Can You Spot the Difference?:
Every picture they post of themselves is taken at their own arm's length away, with a friend under their left arm, and the exact same smile on their face. Every, single, picture.

Where's a Photographer When You Need One:
The only time they won't have their camera is when you actually need one. Then they'll proceed to whine and bitch about it for the rest of the night. While they won't stop longing for their camera, you'll start longing for a gun.

Stop The Presses!:
Pictures from your birthday party are online before the party is over. Camera Queens spend more time working on their clever photo comments than their term papers. Wonder what they did this weekend? Just check their facebook. It's all there in black and white... and color.

Money Mamas

Originally referred to as "Spoiled Bitches," Money Mamas are one of the ones to be wary of. These girls never wear two things: items by a designer you can pronounce, and the same clothes twice. Yeah, so what if they're only twenty and in college? It's really important for them to be in style and chic. They're showing how much more mature than you they are by spending ninety-eight percent of their income on apparel. They call their fathers "Daddy" and their mothers on the weekend. Steer clear fellas. No sense in dishing out a hundred and twenty bucks on a date, just for a chance to go down on a girl.

DEAD GIVEAWAYS:

Is That *Real* Baby Skin?:

Their purses are made only from the finest material, so try and be overly cautious around them. Accidentally spilling your drink on their new lipstick holder could cause them to hate you for life. Seriously.

Get Into My Car:

Good topics of conversation include: what car you drive, the weather, and what car you drive. If they ask this before your name, just tell them it's the Ferrari out front, but they're gonna have to squeeze in the back if they want a ride. Prettiest girls in the front, you understand.

I Got My BA In BJs:

If marrying a man is part of their career plan, this is not the type of girl for you. Unless you yourself are well educated, rich, and extremely unattractive, stay away. Anyone that's counting on manipulating someone into providing for them the rest of their life is obviously not interested in you or your Star Wars action-figure collection.

Goth Gals

Goth Gals have all the fun. Too bad they're not allowed to smile. Being a Goth Gal takes a lot more than blank depressive stares and self-inflicted penknife cuts. It's about hating everything. It's about being completely different by acting like every other gothic kid before them. It's about forming isolated groups resembling black holes in the cafeteria and mingling with the odd balls. It's about having pale skin and purple hair. It's about horrific displays of PDA, just to stick it to the "normies." Most of all, it's about black.

GOTHTARD IS THE NEW BLACK

DEAD GIVEAWAYS:

Black is Back:

They like their coffee black. Just like their clothes, *black*. Just like their fingernails, *black*. Just like their poetry, *black*.

Those Really Stupid Shirts:

They wear shirts that have sloppy hand-written messages printed on them saying things like, "My Brain Made Me Do It" and "Warning: Do Not Feed This Animal." I'm not sure if they're supposed to be funny or scary, because they're neither.

I Met This Girl Online and She Totally Cast a Level 4 Spell On Me:

They're on an *ever quest* for companionship in all the wrong places. Or maybe they are the right places… for them. It's a world of love and warcraft out there that is not easily navigated. Massive Online Gaming is the new nightclub where nerds and Goths can be their normal Timbermaw Furbolgs selves. If you understood that reference, quit reading about yourself.

Don't Know Much About...
ENGLISH

Essential Internet Abbreviations:

<3 – Heart or Love
"I <3 dollar margarita night at BDub's"

ASL? – what is your age/sex/location?
"He had me at ASL"

BRB – Be right back
*"Ah sh*t, my EasyMac is on fire. BRB."*

BTW – By the way
"No, I understand. I'll find another date. Oh, BTW… You're really a fat bitch."

CYA – See ya
"I jussst got home. Ugh. Too tired, too hung over. Passing out. CYA."

GTG – Got to go
*"Oh sh*t. GTG. Everyone's waiting on me downstairs."*

IM me – Instant Message me
"I don't have a pen on me. Can you just IM me when you get home?"

IMO – In my opinion
"Well, IMO I think we should make the party clothing optional."

JK – Just kidding

"I e-mailed everyone those nude pictures of us. JK, I deleted them. Hah, JK again."

NSFW – not suitable for work

"You get the email of the girl & the beer bottle? Careful, its totally NSFW."

OMFG – oh my f'n god

"Our semester projects are due today?! OMFG I'm so screwed."

POS – piece of sh*t (college level)

"Yeah, we got some POS apartment off Roberts St."

POS – parents over shoulder (high school level)

"Oh, yeah... let me just take off my bra and... whoops! Stop. POS!"

THX – Thanks.

"You already bought beer? Thx, man. What do I owe you?"

WTF – What the f#@k?!

"WTF is this I hear about you joining the Army? You know they drug test, right?"

The LOL: Levels Of Laughter

LOL – Laugh Out Loud

"You ate out of that lunchbox you'd never seen before? LOL"

LMAO – Laughing My Ass Off

"You ate out of that old cheesecake box that fell on the floor? LMAO."

ROFL – Rolling On Floor Laughing

"You ate eggs out of that old bird's nest and then three more?! ROFL."

ROFLMAO – Rolling On Floor Laughing My Ass Off

"You ate out that old grandma that claimed to be an ex-whore?! ROFLMAO."

*Can't find it? For a more comprehensive list of acronyms check out Van's BRB 2 IMU.

Conjunction Function:

Like:

These days "like" is now being used to combine any two efforts in verbal communication. It can be placed after any train of thought to connect it to the next feeling described.

Example: "I know I could nail her if I wanted, but like every time I try she runs."

It is also used to describe what was said, exactly how someone acted in the moment, or what said person is thinking.

Example: "He wanted me to drink it, but I was like, no way man. And he was like, do it, ya know. And so I was like, you know what, this ain't even worth it. So I did it, and everyone was like, dammn! But I like, didn't even rub it in his face afterwards, cause he was all like, whatever.

I Know Right:

The old days of simply agreeing with someone are gone. Now we can not only agree with someone that the information is correct, but then concur with them that their personal opinion on the matter is similar to that of our own.

Old Way:

X: "Man, Jimmy thinks he can talk that way to everyone. He doesn't even understand how hard I could whip his ass, either."

Y: "I agree, he does think that. I'm sure you could beat him in a fight too."

New Way:

X: "Man, Jimmy thinks he can talk that way to everyone. He doesn't even understand how hard I could whip his ass, either."

Y: "I know right."

VanWilderism #75
Why don't you just save that for your blog? – And I'll read it later.
Write that down.

Don't Know Much About...
MATH

Yeast + Hops = Beer

Yeast + Sugary Plant = Liquor

Yeast + Grapes = Wine

1 beer = 12 oz.

1 shot = 1.5 oz.

1 glass of wine = 5 oz.

Beer = 4% to 8% alcohol

Liquor = 40% to 55% alcohol

Wine = 10% to 22% alcohol

1 beer = 1 shot = 1 glass of wine

1 keg = 164 beers

1 lbs. = 16 ounces

QP = 4 ounces

Onion or Zip = 1 ounce

1 ounce = (4) quarters

1 quarter = (2) eighths

1 eighth = 3.5 grams

1 baggie (w/o zipper) = 1.1 grams

2 People = Company

3 People = a Crowd

My Fist + Your Face = Knuckle Sandwich

Stupid Guy + Stupid Girl = Pregnancy

Her Legs ÷ Your Hands = Restraining Order

A Party ± Alcohol = Fun%

Bottles ≥ Cans

Meal Plans ≤ Real Food

Campus Dining ≠ Home Cooked

"Your School > Every Other School

Student Loans = Hell

Minutes Spent In Jail = ∞

VanWilderism #51
Don't put all your eggs in one basket, unless you're at the grocery store.
Write that down.

Don't Know Much About...
SCIENCE

There's only one category of Science you'll carry with you for the rest of you life...

Mixology: The Fantastic Formulae
If she asks what's in it, you'd better know!

Mojito
- 2-3 oz Light rum
- Juice of 1 Lime (1 oz)
- 2 tsp Sugar
- 2-4 Mint sprigs
- Soda water

Long Island Iced Tea
- 1 part Vodka
- 1 part Tequila
- 1 part Rum
- 1 part Gin
- 1 part Triple sec
- 1 1/2 part Sour mix
- 1 splash of Coke

Screwdriver
- 2 oz Vodka
- Orange juice

Cosmopolitan
- 1 oz Vodka
- 1/2 oz Triple sec
- 1/2 oz Rose's limejuice
- 1/2 oz Cranberry juice

Sangria
- 1.5L Cabernet Sauvignon
- 1 cup Sugar
- 1 large Lemon, sliced
- 1 large Orange, sliced
- 1 large Apple, sliced
- 3-4 oz plain Brandy
- Soda water

White Russian
- 2 oz Vodka
- 1 oz Coffee liqueur
- Light cream

Margarita
- 1 1/2 oz Tequila
- 1/2 oz Triple sec
- 1 oz Lime juice
- Salt

Alabama Slamma
- 1 oz Southern Comfort
- 1 oz Amaretto
- 1/2 oz Sloe gin
- 1 dash Lemon juice

Sex on the Beach
- 1 oz Vodka
- 3/4 oz Peach schnapps
- Cranberry juice
- Grapefruit juice

Tequila Sunrise
- 2 measures Tequila
- Orange juice
- 2 dashes Grenadine

Bloody Mary
- 1 1/2 oz Vodka
- 3 oz Tomato juice
- 1 dash Lemon juice
- 1/2 tsp Worcestershire
- 2-3 drops Tabasco sauce
- 1 wedge Lime

Redheaded Slut
- 1 1/2 oz Jägermeister
- 1 1/2 oz Peach schnapps
- Fill with Cranberry juice

Liquid Cocaine
- 1/4 shot Grand Marnier
- 1/4 shot SoCo
- 1/4 shot Vodka (Absolut)
- 1/4 shot Amaretto
- 1 splash Pineapple juice

Bahama Mama
- 1/4 oz Coffee liqueur
- 1/2 oz Dark rum
- 1/2 oz Coconut liqueur
- 1/4 oz 151 proof rum
- Juice of 1/2 Lemon
- 4 oz Pineapple juice

Hot Toddy
- 1 tblsp Honey
- 3/4 glass Tea
- 2 shots Brandy
- 1 slice Lemon

Afganistani Whore
- 4 oz Rum
- 1 can Root beer
- 4 oz Vodka

Tom Collins
- 2 oz Gin
- 1 oz Lemon juice
- 1 tsp superfine Sugar
- 3 oz Club soda
- 1 Maraschino cherry
- 1 Orange slice

VanWilderism #117
Having a green thumb is better
than a brown one.
Write that down.

Don't Know Much About...
U.S. HISTORY

U.S. Presidents:

1st – George Washington (Mr. $1 Bill, and quarter)

3rd – Thomas Jefferson (Mr. $2 Bill, and nickel)

7th – Andrew Jackson (Mr. $20 Bill)

16th – Abraham Lincoln (Mr. $5 Bill, and penny)

18th – Ulysses S. Grant (Mr. $50 Bill)

22nd and 24th – Grover Cleveland (Mr. Two Timer)

26th – Teddy Roosevelt (Mr. Ruff Rider)

28th – Woodrow Wilson (Mr. $100K Bill)

32nd – Franklin D. Roosevelt (F.D.R. or Mr. Wheelchair)

35th – John F. Kennedy (Mr. Half-Dollar or Half-Head)

37th – Richard Nixon (Mr. Tricky Dicky)

42nd – Bill Clinton (Mr. I Didn't Do It, Okay I Did)

43rd – George W. Bush (Mr. Dumbass)

Ben Franklin was not a U.S. President, yet appears on the $100 bill.

Wars:

American Civil War (1861-1865) – Part of us won, part of us lost. Thankfully, the South won't rise again.

The First World War (1914-1918) – Allied Powers vs. Central Powers. Allied Powers win but Germany holds a nasty grudge.

The Second World War (1939-1945) – Allied Powers vs. Axis Powers. Allied Powers win again. We lose more lives than Super Mario at a blind gamers' convention.

Gulf War (1990-1991) – USA butts heads with Iraq to liberate Kuwait. Desert-camo becomes all the rage.

Operation Enduring Freedom (2001-present) – USA vs. Al Qaeda. Thought to be the spark igniting the Revolutionary War of 2012, or US Citizens vs. The Patriot Act.

The Past 30 Years:

1976 – The VHS tape is born.

1977 – *Star Wars* gives nerds something to talk about.

1978 – *Animal House* changes college campuses forever.

1979 – The Walkman starts moving.

1980 – The U.S. has a hockey team? The U.S. has a hockey team!

1981 – People want their MTV.

1982 – Phoebe Cates and slow-motion nudity make that whole VHS thing worthwhile.

1983 – Thanks to Scarface, people discover coke and cool coincidentally start with the letter "C."

1984 – If you don't wanna die, keep the wallet and give me the Air Jordans.

1985 – Tyson throws his first official punch, twelve years before he officially eats his first ear.

1986 – Alongside Maverick and IceMan, Goose becomes a respectable nickname.

1987 – Rambo makes headbands cool.

1988 – Steve Hawking proves just because he can't spray it, doesn't mean he can't say it.

1989 – East Berlin knocks down a wall. Proves destruction of public property can be positive.

1990 – D.C. Mayor Marion Barry actually says, "bitch set me up."

His political future is seemingly unhurt.

1991 – Jeffrey Dahmer changes the way America eats.

1992 – Bush Sr. barfs on Japan Prime Minister. Something is lost in the translation.

1993 – Beavis and Butthead make 20 million kids feel normal. Uhh, huh-huh.

1994 – O.J. Simpson's white bronco drives for hours. He's clearly an innocent man.

1995 – Jenny Jones gets a man killed. Amazingly the death isn't from viewing her show.

1996 – America becomes infected by mad cow disease and Jackie Chan.

1997 – South Park and Pam and Tommy's Sex Tape provide entertainment for all ages.

1998 – NASCAR great, Dale Earnhardt dies. One down, fifty to go.

1999 – Napster makes computers useful to teens for the first time, excluding that whole porn thing.

2000 – Slim Shady makes rhymes about killing women to prove he's really tough.

2001 – The iPod gives life a soundtrack, and competitors a headache.

2002 – GTA makes everyone want to steal a car, if they weren't too busy playing game.

2003 – Siegfried and Roy actually do something people want to see.

2004 – The Curse of the Bambino ends. Sox fans everywhere decide life *is* worth living.

VanWilderism #3
Never bite off more than you can spew.
Write that down.

2005 – YouTube gives you control over what you watch. Somehow, Carrot Top survives.

2006 – In response to rumors that he's losing his edge, Vice President Cheney shoots friend in face.

2007 – This book is printed. Nothing else of historical significance happens.

Don't Know Much About...
POLITICS

Suffer and Rage Make Suffrage:

Understanding America's political system can help you hold your head above water at heated dinner table debates, but you need to use the knowledge you learn to see change. You must exercise your right to vote if you want to make a microscopic difference. Luckily for us, our grandparents did all the picketing so we'd have the right to wear those little *I Voted* stickers, making us feel more mature.

Today, everyone besides convicted felons and the mentally handicapped can vote. Now since most voters are criminals or intellectually handicapped and our elections are fixed anyway, you might be wondering: why even vote? This is a very good question that has yet to be answered. Surveys were sent to over a million young voters, age 18-24, to try and find the reasoning behind the weak youth interest. Unfortunately, due to an oversight by the surveyors, the questionnaires were given out during a *Real World* marathon and sadly none were returned.

Puffy said we'd die if we didn't vote. Guess what? Nothing changed. The polls showed the same 18 to 24 year-old turn out as it did in the 60s. The problem with politics is that it's ruining today's entertainment world. I'm not talking about the lawmakers, or even the President. I'm talking about all the artists that try to pound their political views in my ears at every show.

"Uh, Hello Cincinnati! Boy, are we glad to be here! Are you guys ready to ROCK!! Yeah?! Okay!!! But first we wanna talk about how much we hate Bush! Yeah! If you like our music you should vote like we do! Rock-n-roll!"

How about you shut the f#@k up and give me my goddamn money's worth. I love paying five times market price on eBay to see the masterminds behind Green Day talk about their views on Statesmanship vs. Unilateralism.

My point is, kids should do their own research and make their own decisions. Just don't forget, no matter how interested you get in politics, it's still right beside religion and favorite sex positions on the list of strictly taboo topics suitable for a first date.

The Powers That Be:

Executive Branch: Home of the executive power, this government branch only has one limb. It happens to be the one our President dangles from.

Legislative Branch: The legislative power comes from Congress, a house divided into two chambers. This bicameral house contains the Senate and the House of Representatives. Upstairs we have the Senate; two members represent each one of our 50 states equally. Yes, even Rhode Island. Downstairs, the House of Representatives represents each state proportionally by its population. We have 100 members in the Senate, 435 in the House of Reps, and 3 in the House of Pain.

Judicial Branch: Power drains down from the Supreme Court and into lower federal courts. The power continues to leak from the federal courts into lower level judiciary systems until there's nothing left but a faint aroma of authority. Cops bathe in this stuff, so make sure to get the hell outta Dodge when you catch a whiff of their clout in the air.

The Best Parties in the US:
(In no particular order)

Republican Party: One of the two major US parties, most college Republicans choose this party "because that's what Daddy is." Republicans think the fact-filled Bible has a place in our government, and that if we keep banning homosexuality it'll eventually go away. They're similar to the Chess Club throwing a 20-kegger fiesta. There are plenty of people in attendance, but damn if it isn't the lamest party you've ever seen.

Democratic Party: The other heavy hitter, Democrats, follow a liberal plan. They want higher minimum wages and lower emission vehicles. They believe we have the right to choose whether an unborn fetus should live or die, but no business playing God with the life of a three-time convicted child molester. At least they try to use the fetuses for that whole stem-cell research thing in favor of a dumpster.

Independent, Reform Party: These guys have the heart of a champion. Like a noseless cripple in a beauty pageant, you can't help but admire their courage and effort. Independents agree a little bit with the Republicans, and a little bit with the Democrats. In all honesty, if you plan on voting for the Independent candidate, you might just as well roll up your vote, stick it in your dick hole, and piss it away. I've always voted for the Libertarian or Independent candidate, but after witnessing the Florida poll debacle, I think I'll just vote for whom I hate the least.

Libertarian Party: Libertarians come in third behind Repubes and Dummycrats with a party that grows in size every year. Currently with over 600 members in office, the Libertarians are no laughing matter. These political bad-asses work for improved civil liberties and lightly regulated, laissez-faire markets. If you're brushing up on your French, laissez-faire means, "let do, let go, let pass."

Green Party: Remember Ralph Nader? The Green Party is just as hippie as they sound. Focusing on environmentalism, and local autonomy. Sounds like a sweet idea if we were all still trading flour for potatoes, but we're not. The Green Party often wins in California and heavily elderly populated areas of Florida where the well-aged voters often mistake the question for "Favorite Color."

VanWilderism #37
Beating around the bush is not good foreplay.
Write that down.

Don't Know Much About... SPORTS

Quit trying to figure out the eight ways to reach first base, because there are twenty-three. There's no need to touch base on the rules, because if you don't know them by now, odds are you never will. Learn these sports milestones and you can survive any meat-headed conversation a frat party can dish out.

Baseball:

September 18, 1919 – White Sox Become Dirty Sox and Agree to Throw 1919 World Series

January 4, 1920 – Bambino is Sold From the Red Sox to the New York Yanks, Giving Boston Fans Everywhere One More Reason to Hate the Yankees

October 30, 1945 – Jackie Robinson Signs With the Brooklyn Dodgers and the Future of 10,000 White Players is Crushed

April 8, 1974 – Hank Aaron Supersedes Babe Ruth as Home Run King with 715, Candy Bar Makers Regret Not Making the Afro-Aarron Chocolate Bar

December 12, 1975 – Reserve Clause Falls as Free Agents and Overpaid Pricks are Born

October 2, 1978 – Bucky F#@kin' Dent is Hated By All

August 23, 1989 – Pete Rose Bets He'll Never Make It Into Baseball's Hall of Fame and Wins

May 1, 1991 – Nolan Ryan Proves Being 44 Just Makes You Look Old On the Outside

September 14, 1994 – Bud Selig Cancels World Series, Baseball Takes New Low Next to Curling

September 27, 1998 – Mark McGwire Homers 70 in One Season, His Balls are Thankful to Still Be Big Enough to See It

Basketball:

March 2, 1962 – Wilt Chamberlain Scores 100 Points in a Single Game, and 200 Women Afterwards

September 10, 1972 – Soviets Beat USA in Basketball, US Responds 'We Were Keeping Score?'

March 29, 1975 – John Wooden Wins Tenth Consecutive NCAA Title, Still Can't Get Laid

March 26, 1979 – Magic and Larry Start College Rivalry, Helping Races Form Friendships Everywhere

April 4, 1983 – NC State Stomps Favored Houston for NCAA Title, March Madness is Born

June 19, 1984 – Michael Jordan is #3 Overall Draft Pick, #1 and #2 Fight for Bulls Season Tickets

Football:

November 19, 1928 – Notre Dame Rallies to Beat Army, The Gipper is Proud, Whoever the Hell That Is

December 28, 1958 – Greatest Game Ever Played, Colts and Giants in Overtime Make Televised Sports Suddenly Worth Watching

February 4, 1959 – Vince Lombardi Made Green Bay Packers Head Coach, Fedoras Become New Rage

January 12, 1969 – 18-Point Underdog Joe Namath Guarantees Victory in Super Bowl and Wins, Somehow This Makes It Okay for Him to Wear Fur Coats and Pantyhose

September 21, 1970 – Howard Cosell's Nose Gives Birth to Monday Night Football

January 14, 1979 – Miami Dolphins Complete NFL's Only Undefeated Season, Then Go On to Lose Next 600 games

December 16, 1973 – O.J. Simpson Breaks 2,000 Yards in a Season, then Rushes for 200 miles in white bronco

November 22, 1984 – Doug Flutie and BC Defeat Miami on Last Desperate Play, Much Similar to Michael Douglas's Pass on Catherine Zeta-Jones

Tennis:

September 29, 1973 – Billie Jean King Defeats Bobby Riggs, People Confused of the Significance of Man Beating Man

July 5, 1980 – John McEnroe Plays Tennis for 4 Hours and Still Loses

Hockey:

February 22, 1980 – US Hockey Team Beats Soviet Union 4-3, First Miracle on Ice That Isn't Labeled Gay

October 15, 1989 – Wayne Gretzky Becomes NHL's All-Time Leading Scorer, Finally Canadian Women Have Someone to Desire

Golf:

April 13, 1986 – Jack Nicklaus, 46, Wins Sixth Masters, Makes Fortune Selling Other Five Jackets

April 13, 1997 – Tiger Woods Becomes Youngest Masters Champ, Club Still Makes Him Use Other Bathroom

Boxing:

June 22, 1938 – Joe Louis Beats Some Schmeling German in 124 Seconds, Hitler Cries

April 27, 1956 – Rocky Marciano Leaves Before He Loses As Undefeated Heavyweight Champ at 49-0

February 25, 1964 – Cassius Clay Knocks the Sh*t Out of Sonny Liston

March 8, 1971 – Ali vs. Frazier I, the Unthinkable Happens as the Greatest Loses by Decision. Ali Comes Back to Beat Frazier Senseless Twice

June 28, 1997 – Mike Tyson Eats Evander Holyfield's Ear on George Forman's Grill

Olympic Records and Others:

July 15, 1912 – Jim Thorpe Becomes World's Greatest Athlete

August 9, 1936 – Jessie Owens Sticks it to the Aryans

May 6, 1954 – Roger Bannister Does Four Minute Mile, KIA Sets New Goal for Cars

October 18, 1969 – Bob Beamon Jumps a Hell of a lot Further Than You Can

September 5, 1972 – 11 Athletes are Murdered at Munich Olympics, Terrorists Banned From Competing

VanWilderism #5
You haven't lived until you've shot-putted blitzed on Jager. *Write that down.*

June 10, 1973 – Secretariat Wins Triple Crown and Beats Stevie Nicks as King of Horses

July 13, 1976 – 14 year-old Nadia Comaneci Lands Perfect 10, Men Everywhere Discover They Have Dirty Minds

August 3, 1984 – Mary Lou Retton Nails a Perfect 10 Once Judges Realize It's Not Beauty Contest

Shape Up Young Man

Along with killing kegs and dazzling dames, keeping yourself in shape should be one of your top priorities. In today's world, everyone and their grandfather have six-pack abs. Not having a washboard stomach, chiseled tri's, or tree trunk thighs could leave you feeling like Rick Moranis at an IronMan competition. Not only is the campus's fitness center free, but you're also in the prime time to start building the physique you want to carry with you the rest of your life. I've compiled a workout plan that should easily fit everyone's hectic schedule.

Legs & Buttocks

Dead Lifts: *(Straighten back, lift with your ass, penguin walk)*
Head to the party a little early. When it's time to get the keg, macho up and get it yourself. Best not done in front of females until you've gotten a handle on the exercise.
More pain more gain: Carry it from the store.

Stair Lunges: *(Begin on the first floor, start by taking two steps up at a time, increase difficulty taking three steps at a time)*
Instead of scrambling for your books every morning, keep all sixteen of them in your backpack at all times. Elevators are off limits, too. Purposefully leave ten minutes later than usual and

try to make the time up by dashing across campus. We've all seen that rat-packing runner before; you can bet your bottom dollar his ass is carved from marble.

More pain more gain: Get rid of your books, start reading bricks.

Shoulders

Vertical Press: *(Stand knees bent facing the wall, catch weight at shoulders and lift, release at maximum height and step back)*

Next time you get out of class early, head over to the standing-yard of your campus's security station. Sign-in as a visitor and find the drunk detainees wandering in the grass. Stand facing the fence about a foot away. With your back to the inmates, yelp the word "out!" and they'll know what to do. When the sound of their dashing footsteps reaches your back, cup your hands beside your shoulders, dip, catch a foot in each hand, and throw weight straight over head. Repeat until a guard comes or someone is caught in the barbed wire.

More pain more gain: Do the same thing, but at a fat camp.

Vertical Lifts or Butterflys: *(Holding weight in each hand, lift arms straight out from sides until they are parallel with ground, then slowly lower)*

Next time you're grabbing beer from your local grocer, take your time leaving after you've found your beer. With a case, or 12-pack in each hand, pretend to be a bird flying around the store while you work your shoulders.

More pain more gain: Navigate the store with two shopping karts. Can't let wheels touch ground.

Chest & Triceps

Bench Press: *(Lie flat on back, press weight straight up away from body to maximum extension, release)*

Sneak over to the dorm of your most over-weight sexually active friend. When you see a girl is coming, hide under the bed. Use your upper arm strength to keep them going and you from dying. Make sure you and your friend have a safe-word in case the bed begins to break.

More pain more gain: Suggest a threesome and buy the pizza.

Biceps

Preacher Curls: *(Palms up, shoulder width apart, lift arms from fully extended to vertical, release)*

Volunteering around campus can be sexy. Pitch in at your pool by helping lift ladies out of the water. Not too fast now, you don't want that top coming off.

More pain more gain: Help lift the lunch ladies onto the public buses.

Standing Curls: *(Palms up, curl right arm up, then release, repeat with left arm)*

Getting the laundry done never felt so good. Pull your laundry bag up onto washer from the floor, and then put it back down. Set to cycle.

More pain more gain: Leave your pockets filled with change when you throw them in the hamper.

Abs

Sit-ups: *(Lie flat on back, knees or legs in air, bring self up from horizontal to vertical as quickly as possible, release)*

Next time you and your girl are hooking up in her dorm, spice it up by crawling in her roommate's bed while she's in class. Every time footsteps approach your door you'll both instantaneously sit straight up. Keep the suspense up until you hear the keys hit the door and switch back over.

More pain more gain: Have her on top.

Relationship Status:
It's Complicated

A recent study surveyed 200,000 students and found the number one most difficult concept for current college students to grasp is, you guessed it, organic chemistry. In a close second we had "relationships." Why do college relationships have to be so damn complicating? You go to the same school, you live within walking distance of each other, you're allowed to spend the nights together, you can walk with one another to class, when you get out of class the other is waiting, when you try to avoid the other they start stalking you even more than they already were. They lurk in bushes around your class, "coincidentally" bump into you all over campus, and have your News Feed on auto-refresh. Weeks after you've ended it they'll come knocking on your door at four in the morning, pretending to want a casual talk, but they really just know you have someone over and want to make some sort of confrontation. Oh yeah, now I remember. Kids are psycho.

If you want a college girlfriend you have to weigh all the evidence. Does she have baggage, or brains, or hairy forearms? Does she weigh more than you, eat more than you, or fart more than you? Are her "guy friends" guy friends, or *guy* friends? Does she dress original or like every girl who went to A&E that weekend. Does she have big goals or big moles? How does she look naked? All these shallow observations must be made, weighed, and laid out under a microscope. Choose your relationships wisely, because you can only test-drive so many cars before the dealer starts banning you from the lot. (NOTE: If you're some sort of super-geek that's never had a date before, feel free to jump into whatever sad, loveless, detrimental relationship you can find.)

When choosing a partner, ask yourself the three basic questions. Number One. Has she slept or hooked up with any of my friends? If the answer is yes, move along. It will come up sometime later, and you won't be able to get over it. Everyone will get involved and then you'll all feel a lot less human for it.

Number Two. What are her interests? If her interests include, "shopping, my BFF, or readin' whan no one is lookin'" – motion to pass. And girls, if his interests include, "Jimmy Fallon, getting in fights, or my abs" – stay away. You'll be surprised how much time you can save yourself by doing a little research. Notice I said *little*. You don't have to backtrack through their entire history of online photos to see whom they've been drunkenly making out with recently. Check the basics and move on. Do they list any of your favorite bands in their favorites? What sort of movies do they enjoy on a rainy Sunday night? Do they list their favorite books, or every book they've ever read? Do people write how much they love them on their wall, or how much of a crazy bitch they are? Do your research, and you'll have no problem solving this case.

Number Three. How do they kiss? If you can't make out with the person for ten hours straight, forget it.

Now lets say you've found the one that's passed all the tests. She hasn't been with any of your buddies (or enemies), you love the same things, and you lock lips more times a day than the FCC. Now you have what we call "too perfect." Because this babe is so great, Murphy's Law states it can't go smoothly. She passed all the tests, so you think you're in love. You've found The One. Now she thinks you're The One. Now you're getting married. What's next? That's right; now you're dead. The only thing that makes me sicker than married couples in school are engaged couples in school. Married couples already ruined it for one another, engaged couples at least have a chance. A chance they'll never take.

Oh, and how they love to use their new monikers. "Hey, this is my fiancé." Every chance they get, "My fiancé this…" and "My fiancé that…"

"Did I ever tell you about the time my fiancé…"

"Yes! And even if you hadn't, I *still* wouldn't care!"

They act all fake lovey to hide their fear that they're stuck with someone equally as pathetic as themselves. Then again, I'm coming off kind of jealous sounding. Go off and have your ugly babies. Throw your lives away, and when it falls through and you're back out in the real world, you'll be traveling it with a tired, worn, and aged body. You'll have half the energy, confidence and pizzazz. It will be a dark and lonely world, and I'll be there, standing over you saying, "I told you so you old miserable fool! Why didn't you listen to me!" It's sad that that's one of my goals in life.

Okay. You've found the perfect gal, the two of you have vowed never to mention the word marriage, and she gives you your space. Life is perfect. What could ever screw this up? Well, that cute blonde that just walked in the door for one.

Yes, you will be the one to screw it up. Give a virgin Jessica Simpson and he will eventually get bored. It's man's natural way of staying a man. If it were easy for us to stay with one woman, women would love us and the roles would be reversed. That being said, I'll sum up all my advice in one sentence. If you want to be with a girl you have to give her 100%, and since you can't do that yet, forget that whole boyfriend/girlfriend model all together. You'll save money, get laid more, and always have an open agenda. The system works; use it, don't abuse it.

VanWilderism #58
You can't wash off skank.
Write that down.

Movies Aren't Real: Common College Misconceptions

Although college-based movies are extremely entertaining to watch, they often setup some pretenses that can be confusing to freshman. I've compiled a list of common movie misconceptions about college to help clarify fact from fiction.

Spying On Girls Is Dangerous,
But Your Boner Won't Be Your Downfall:

No matter how much of an animal house you come from, you don't have to always act like a baboon. While climbing up a ladder to catch some sorority sweethearts in their birthday suits seems like a great idea, it's not going to be your boner that pushes you off that ladder. It will be the cops, or worse, a local meathead who is coming to pick up your eye-candy. Just stay off ladders and keep your stalking confined to the Internet.

Nerds CAN Be Cool:

If a Nerd wants revenge, they will get it. *False.*

Nerds always end up winning in the end. *False.*

Nerds score with the babes, throw the best parties, and beat out the jocks. *False.*

To this day they're still arguing at the video store over whether this movie should go under Comedy or Fantasy. Whatever frat looks the lamest is the lamest. There is no hidden ray of hope here; what you see is what you get.

Divided We Shall Fall:
Politically correct universities show us college is composed of more whack groups than a fourteen-year-old's iPod, but they're not quite as hardcore as portrayed. Most activists join for the novelty of it and the vegetarians don't dress like Eddie Vedder.

That's One Smart Cookie Cleaner Upper:
Your janitor is never going to solve math problems faster than you. If he does, it's time the two of you switch roles. And if you are that low on the intelligence scale, then you'll soon learn the true meaning of *"goodwill"* hunting, dumpster diving, and penny panhandling.

The Big Test:
So you're really hanging by a thread on the whole graduation thing, huh? Don't worry, I'm sure all your professors won't mind reinventing the requirements of a diploma and making one giant comprehensive test you'll miraculously be able to pass. I've seen this at least four times in movies, and zero times in what I'd call "the real world." Study hard, kids.

DumbLine:
You think band competitions are intense on screen? No really, I'm asking. Because if Nick Cannon can't make something look fun on the big screen, how in the hell is it ever going to be fun in your gymnasium? That's right, it's not.

Aw Man, You Invited Your Kid Again?:
If one of your parents should ever decide to enroll at your university, I guarantee they won't be helping you make more friends. Heed my advice and pretend you don't know them; at least until you need to hit them up for that laundry they wash and fold so nicely.

We're Really Old School:

Any man over thirty is not going to be cool. They're not going to throw the sickest parties, and they're not going to win over the hearts of the local lasses. They will undoubtedly make every girl they talk to uncomfortable enough to finger their rape whistle, and every guy ask, "What are you, like 40?" Then they'll smile uneasily, slip back into the crowd, and stare at breasts until they're eventually escorted out the door.

Get With The Program Son:

Sure your head coach looks mean from the sidelines, but he's not the maniac he appears to be. In real life players don't practice drills in-between traffic, and they're never going to put in the little guy, so quit asking.

Road Tripping With Your Three Favorite Allies:

Your road trip will never be as exciting as the movies so don't even bother comparing them. You're not jumping a ditch. You're not stealing a bus. You're not getting laid.

Get Wilder:

I hate to admit, but you're no Van Wilder. Your folks aren't paying for eight years of school unless it comes with two BA's and an MFA. If you want to stay, you gotta pay. Two words: Student loans.

January, February, March, April Fools: Pranks and Shams for Any Occasion

Anytime, Anywhere.

You can do these deeds whenever you so please.

Hey Shrimp, Sit Up Straight:

First you'll need a pound of shrimp. Then all you'll need is for your least favorite neighbor to leave his desk unattended. Go into his room and remove the seat of his swivel chair from its base. Fill the chair's base cylinder with the shrimp and reattach the chair. Give it a few weeks and play stupid when everyone suddenly wants to hangout in your room and not his.

Ah, Baloney:

Don't you hate those kids coming into college with new cars that cost more than their tuition? Lucky for you, I do, too. Next time you're walking by that prized ride, toss an uneaten piece of Oscar Mayer on it. If it's a hot enough day, the acids in the baloney will react with the heat and eat a perfect hole through the paint. Be a good guy and toss several pieces to give the car that sleek, polka-dotty feel.

Animal House:

Release five pigs or rats in your school. Label each one 1, 2, 4, 6, and 9. Watch the janitors roam campus looking for that tricky number 7.

Don't Have a Cow:

If by the grace of God you should ever find a cow, lead it upstairs. Walk it to the highest floor on campus and leave it. That's the prank. Cows can't walk downstairs.

It's Alive, It's Alive!:

Freeze shaving cream. Saw off top. Throw the frozen can-shaped blobs anywhere and everywhere. As they unfreeze they will expand, and expand, and expand. Four or five cans can fill an entire freshman dorm room.

Aw, Look. He's Sleeping.

Why you should learn to sleep with your eyes open…

What a Dickhead:

Yeah, just draw a dick on his face. Now add some balls. Now a little bit of shaving cream. Now some honey. Hey, don't you keep some chocolate syrup in the pantry?

I Touch Myself:

So they passed out like a little angel. Time to make them a little devil. Place one hand down their pants, one hand down your pants, and one butt-crack in their face. Smile for the camera!

Bed Fit For a King:

Replace the slats of your roommate's bed with tape or dental floss. Whatever you can find that's strong enough to hold the weight of the mattress. Wait for you roommate to spring into bed, and through the other side.

No Bathroom is Safe.

And you thought pee and poo were funny before!

Seat Mister:

Saran Wrap the toilet bowl. Don't use.

It's Hot, No It's Cold:

Icy-hot the toilet seat.

The Hair Up There:

Empty out your mate's Pro-V and replace it with Nair. He'll think it's really, really funny.

Bloody Stool:

Take your unused ketchup and hot sauce packets and gently place them under toilet seats. When someone sits down they'll splat the back of their knees or ass.

But They Locked Me Out.
Locked out? Never fear.

There's plenty of damage you can do through a door crack.

Cream Room:

Fill a manila envelope with shaving cream. Slide the opening of the envelope under the door and stomp. The room will be instantly covered in shaving cream.

Ghost Story:

Like a cream room, sneak up to the locked door. This time come when your target is sleeping. Pour a whole bag of flour at the bottom of the door and blow through with any old hairdryer. If done correctly, every square inch of your ex-friend's room should have a layer of white powder on it.

Knock, Knock, Popcorn:

First you'll need to go to your local mass food supplier and by a 50-pack of microwavable popcorn bags. While one of you pops popcorn, the other should start taping together a mock door made of printer paper. Make it about a foot shorter than the mark's door, and half a foot wider. Once the bags are popped, empty them all into a garbage bag. Tape your faux door around the doorframe, making it flush at the bottom, leaving a few inches of space between the door and the paper wall. Fill the void with the popped popcorn. It should appear to be an oddly buttery, giant white sheet over the door to passers by. Knock on the top of the door. The unsuspecting fool on the inside will open up to a sea of Mr. Redenbacher's finest.

VanWilderism #27

For every "this year" there will always be a "next year."
Write that down.

Babes and Dweebs: The Only Two Types of People

The shift from High School to College can be a dramatic one. On one hand, you'll be introduced to a plethora of personalities (see the *Too Clichéd* section). On the other hand, all these people are either one type of personality or the other: a babe or a dweeb. Now your friends are your friends, and your family is your family. They have names and stories and little individual traits you've grown to know. They aren't exactly categorized into this babe/dweeb folder because you know them on a personal level. Everyone else is a different story. There are also exceptions, but I'll get into that later.

First off, let's lay down the basic foundation for this dweeb/babe structure we're going to build upon. Anyone of the opposite sex is a babe. Everyone that shares your gender is a dweeb. It's a pretty straightforward system. Once you make contact with said babe or dweeb they can be transformed into a friend with a name. This also works in reverse. Attractive female friends can have names, but also can be permanently labeled a babe due to their parents' favorable genes. That being said, guys you know on a first name basis can also be labeled a permanent dweeb if they act the role. It all seems very confusing at first, but time and practice can quickly sort it all out.

So what does it mean to be a babe? Simply stated, it means you're a possible sex partner. Emphasis on the word: *possible.* It's

possible to see some babes coming down the street, but as they come into better focus you realize you wouldn't like to make their acquaintance. Now, these girls aren't changed from their status as a babe. There are all kinds of babes. Beautiful babes and butch babes aren't too far apart in the slang dictionary. What changes is your inflection of the word "babe" which is directly proportional to the level of hotness in the aforementioned babe.

The same can be said for dweebs. Due to the fact that most guys don't go around straining their necks trying to check out every cool looking dude they see, every other male they come across should be considered a dweeb until he proves himself otherwise. You see some guys sitting at the table where you and your buds had planned to sit? First thing your brain says, "Who the hell are these dweebs?" As rude or ignorant as it sounds, that's the way it should be. If guys went around expecting every other group of guys they encountered to be as cool as their friends, we as men would all have a lot of trouble justifying why we tend to stick around the same losers we've developed lifelong friendships with.

Since we're all entitled to our own opinions I can't tell you whom you're going to mesh with. Everyone has a different flavor they prefer and that's the way it should be. In my book, the transformation process from dweeb to friend is a difficult one. In all honesty, most of my "acquaintance-friends" are dweebs and just don't know it. The select five or six that have passed the "best-friend" test did it subconsciously and over the duration of our very long and testing friendship.

You'll have to walk this road alone if you want to make it to the other side. Always be judgmental, but never show it. Never forget other's mistakes, but never hold it against them. Finally, make friends with babes. Babes know babes who know more babes. Oh yeah, and don't call them babes. They tend to hate that.

NOTE: There can also be dweeby-babes, but that's a whole other chapter all together.

Piss On Your Neighbors

I've found that the key to leading a happy life throughout college is not only loving where you live, but also loving those you live around. Having great neighbors can easily shift any lousy day into a relaxing night. I used to love coming home to find the guys downstairs having a BBQ, or that hot single mom upstairs needing help laying some carpet. But what about those unlucky few who don't have intimate connections with their next-door dwellers? What about all the people that hate their nasty neighbors? Most people would tell you to kill them with kindness, since odds are you're the new kid on the block, coming into their territory. I say, f#@k 'em.

Like a fine wine, college only gets better with time. Freshman year I was living the easy life in the dorms. By second semester an ongoing dispute with my vampire-obsessed chronic-masturbating roommate turned ugly and the Park's residential advisor sent me packing. I was moved into a nearby dorm room that was coincidently located adjacent to where my best friend on campus lived, whom I'll refer to as Pattyson. As freshman year rolled to halt, Pattyson and I planned out our sophomore living situation. We found a suitable trailer located on campus and moved in the next year. It was a real sh*t-hole but we loved it. Our trailer-mates weren't too bad either. Not too bad that is, if you could get over one's excessive hair shedding and the other's pungent body odor that evoked images of a dying beached whale scatting rotten Indian food.

For our junior year we decided to step it up another notch and move into an apartment located right off the edge of campus. The location was perfect, but all of our neighbors appeared significantly older. One night when some neighboring girls that lived a few houses down came over, everything changed. We were out on our second floor balcony enjoying a few cocktails and some grass when I tried placing the pipe on our pitched balustrade. Unlike the rooster laying an egg on the barn roof, this riddle had an answer. The glass piece rolled away from the deck and down into the soft uncut grass below. Since it was my pipe, my house, and my fault, I gladly volunteered to go retrieve the fallen bowl.

The twenty second walk outside and downstairs left me with the urge to relieve myself. Seeing how the efficiency below us was dark and lifeless as always, it looked like the perfect place to break the seal. Growing up on a farm and consistently pissing outside my entire life had granted me with a very powerful stream. While most guys were holding back to avoid urinal re-splash, I was trying to make it to the other side of our dirt road. I pelted the apartment's full-glass backdoors like a sprinkler on Sunday morning. The hypnotic sound of liquid on glass in the pitch-black night could have put me to sleep if it wasn't so abruptly interrupted. The liquid wasn't bouncing off glass anymore, but something that sounded a bit more like denim.

"What the hell are you doing?!" a voice boomed as the door ripped open.

I would have told him "running away" had I not already been bouncing back up the stairs, and into my apartment. I had barely shut my door when a pounding knock came. I opened the door as cool as a cucumber, trying to muffle my panting by wheezing heavily through my nose.

"Oh, hello." *(wheeze)* "What's going on, man?" I casually propped my elbow in the door's archway.

"Where is he?" the neighbor snapped in piss-soaked pants.

Looking him over, I felt sorry for what I'd done. Dogs didn't even treat trees this bad. I also felt a little disgusted. The man had rushed up to our door before showering or even changing clothes.

"Where's who?" I was playing dumb.

"You know who. I saw him run away and followed his wet footsteps to your door."

"Umm, let me think," I said trying to buy time. He wasn't having it.

"That's it, I'm calling the cops. I know what he looks like." Then he marched back down the stairs as proudly as any grown-man drenched in urine could.

His last statement made it obvious he didn't get a good look at me, but our houseguests still found this to be an opportune time to leave. Pattyson and I sat around and killed beers until the pigs arrived. As always, the cops seemed more amused by the situation than agitated. I told them the kid had run off into the woods, but I wouldn't mind cleaning up the mess. While I sat there on my hands and knees soaking up the urine, Pattyson and the officers discussed their own theories. Pattyson stayed true to my story, but the cops weren't born yesterday. It doesn't take the Hardy Boys to figure out that if someone pisses all over a patio, no one else is going to willingly clean it up, except the culprit himself. I finished the job and was released to my bed.

By the end of the week, our downstairs urinal-cake couple was moving on to bigger and better things.

"So you guys moving?" I asked.

"Eat sh*t, Spady." And that was that.

What good was accomplished by this episode? The next day a couple of fellow college students were moving in. Friendships were formed, and adventures had. One of the guys ended up becoming one of my close friends, and followed Pattyson and me into our townhouse senior year.

So your neighbor's a douche. Big deal. Piss on them... until someone you like moves in. You don't need to do it my way, but you need to do it. Life is about actions and reactions. Sit around and nothing will happen. I guarantee it.

On an ending note: as effective as this method is, it sadly does not work on professors, parents or girlfriends. You'll have to resort to old school verbal communication skills to get those stones rolling.

VanWilderism #200
Don't break a deal by breaking the seal... hold your pee until the time is right. *Write that down.*

Road Tripping:
The List and The City

When the time comes, and it will, you'll be pushed out of your safe little nest hidden high within the lush branches of your sheltered tree and forced to try out your wings for the first time as you plummet towards the earth. Now you may have felt this when you left home and went to college. You may have experienced something similar on a spring break trip you took to the Caymans. Whenever it was, if it wasn't a *real* impromptu road trip, you didn't get the full-framed picture.

Not much of a traveler myself, my first *real* road trip wasn't until I was in college. I had made some weekend journeys with friends in high school, going to concerts in neighboring states, but nothing too big. To satiate my appetite for new culture outside my small farm town, I decided to take a trip to the Big Apple.

The morning came like a rainstorm. We packed our meager belongings: a corduroy backpack, one cracked brown plastic suitcase, two pairs of shoes to compensate for the flip-flops on our feet, a glass pipe, two bags of grass, fifth a Jack, case of beer and one pack of cigarettes. David's truck was a real piece. We talked most of the ride. About our 'things to do before we die' list. About what things involved NYC and how we would accomplish them. We talked about how this trip would inspire and alter our perspective on the future. How it was our sort of Mecca. We talked about women and what we had recently been reading. While studying Hemingway, I had just read a story on how Hunter Thompson had gone to Hemingway's mountain home to get a more gonzo journalistic feel on the man he was writing about. He saw huge elk horns nailed above Hemingway's door, the man he had been studying exclusively for years. He grabbed the horns, ripped them off the wood and ran. Being one of my idols at the time, I envied the situations Thompson found himself in and his fortitude for getting himself out.

David had driven for over three hours and wanted me to drive into the City, so we switched 45 minutes out. Getting in the City proved to take just as long as getting there, so our time behind the wheel ended up being about equal. We were staying with my friend at the time whose name I won't mention. His apartment was a real dive in the upper-east side of Spanish Harlem. He had grown a beard. You could walk up on the roof, drink a 40 ounce and throw it down onto the train tracks below, with the smashes bouncing off every building. These people didn't even hear it. They didn't hear the horns, the police sirens at 3:00 am, the bottles, the screams, or the gunshots. Their ears are callused over from life in the City. I envied them. Even then, two hours in, I could feel the City growing in me. I was breathing it in deep through my lungs and into my bloodstream, straight into my heart. I dropped my bottle onto the roof of a car, barely missing the only person on the whole block.

"What the hell are you doing?" my bearded friend asked. I didn't know. I was being reckless, which wasn't necessarily out of the norm, but I felt surreal.

"I don't know man," I said.

At least I was honest. The bottle barely missed the loafer's head, misting him with glass. Instead of frightening him, it intrigued the streetwalker. The homeless love interaction. Love the thought of anyone wanting to make any form of contact with them, even if it was by chucking a glass bottle at them from nine stories up. David and The Beard peered over and quickly lurched back. What was so scary about him? He should be the one scared. Now I was intrigued. I squatted to half and leaned over the twenty four-inch sidewall. The wall was just high enough to look like it would trip you, sending you helplessly to the Manhattan sidewalks. I felt a magnetic pull standing near it. An unseen inertia could be felt, making me feel dizzy, getting pulled closer to the edge. Vertigo. I swore I felt my feet sliding in the gravel, trying to take grip. I took a tug-of-war stance, placing my left leg firmly up against the siding and all my weight on my back right foot. I saw the man on the sidewalk. I stared at him looking up at us, gesturing something. I couldn't make him out. The focus on his body suddenly snapped into vision when I realized he was pointing at me, directly between my eyes. I fell back dumbfounded onto the loose stone roof. What is it about this City and this power it gives people? I wanted to see more.

The next morning I woke to a 200-ton iron train rumbling past our window. 'Awesome' I thought. No one else seemed to notice. It was even worse during rush hour. The Beard was up, coming out of a shower that looked like it made you dirtier. Yawning I could touch the wall to each side of me simultaneously. I hang my shirts in a room bigger than this back home and pay half the rent. 'Awesome' I thought. I was getting a crush on the City. The Beard thought I was weird for asking him questions like; "Should I really wear my wallet in my front pocket?" "No eye contact right?" "Just get an All-Day subway pass, no taxis?" He answered with strange looks from an unimpressed eye. He thought I was better than that.

The Beard went to work. He has a job walking dogs for eight dollars an hour. Meanwhile David and I checked out our list of goals. We ate a hog dog at Yankees stadium. Check #37. Smoked a jaybird in Times Square. Check #42. Shot a bottle cap off the

Empire State building. Check #47. Took a piss in Central Park. Check #28. After that we headed towards a local favorite in Spanish Harlem. We had ninety-six dollars worth of tequila. I pissed on a phone booth on the corner of 86th and Park. That wasn't even on the list. We met back up with the Beard. He had just got done walking Cyndi Lauper's dog.

"Whoa, you walk Cyndi Lauper's dog!?" I said.

"Not Cindy Crawford, Cyndi Lauper." He said.

I was thinking of Cindy Crawford. I didn't really care either way. The City was taking hold. I asked if he had keys. He told me I'd never get in there. I'd never make it past security. She lived in an upscale condo complex across Brooklyn. Everyone that lived there probably made more money than her.

I just walked in the front doors. They suspected that I lived there just like everyone else. Just like I thought. I came to the door. 7-A. There was an A and B on each floor, but I never saw a C or D. I knew inside would be huge. The key worked; the Beard was no bullsh*t. I moved inside. The twenty foot long blush pink hallway was covered with various priceless memorabilia lined with a mother of pearl mahogany trim that led to a foyer. Nineteen feet in I heard someone walking towards me. I froze. I couldn't move. In fight or flight I guess I'm fright. It's an instinctual trait past down from our great ancestors. If I was in the jungle and a tiger walked by, I'd have to be completely still. Now we do it on instinct; become stiller than anyone could possibly physically do alone. My veins burned I was so still, trying to move so hard. The harder I pushed the harder my body flamed. I saw a shadow come and go and that was enough. I finally got some sort of control and flew. I moved like my wings were clipped. My knees felt like they were in a cast, unable to bend, thighs rock hard. Hobbling as if I was severely injured, I made my way back from were I'd come. On the way out I saw her Gold Album for 'She's So Unusual'. Hardly my elk horns, but I grabbed it. It fit perfectly in my corduroy backpack since I had unloaded all my personal effects on the Beard's futon before coming. I took the stairs down, half a floor per stride.

Thankfully, I had achieved an amateurish understanding of the subway system. I took the 7 to grand central and the 6 to 103rd from there. I was back at the Beard's place in 40 minutes. We laughed about it on the roof.

I felt different. I could do anything. I couldn't even remember why this trip was my Mecca. The City's customs had taken hold of me: the graffiti everywhere, the bums pissing on churches, the rats the size of cats.

We left the next morning. The drive back was quiet. Some sorry voter in front of us at a Shell station drove off with the gas nozzle still in his tank. We just solemnly watched it happen. Watched them forget. Quietly watched. The nozzle separated at the top. Gas splashed the front of our truck. David smiled a bit. So did I. We were out of the City now.

VanWilderism #286
Ride the horse that you came in on.
Write that down.

THAT'S ABOUT IT

Grocery Shopping At 7-Eleven For The Health Conscious

So you have a 14-plus-flex meal plan, good for you, seriously it's good to have meals and it's good to have a plan. Let's do the math on that one though, okay, Timmy? That's lunch plus dinner seven times a week filled with yummy salt, sugars, fat (is there really any fat that you can call your friend? – I don't think so), and enough carbohydrates to choke even the most intrepid of orally fixated sophomoric co-eds with an eating disorder. A side note here: girls it's great to practice your gag reflex but there are times the body is meant to actually do what it's designed to do. Take it from Ms. PacMan... she's cute, she's fun, and she swallows.

**SNACKS
ARE GOOD**

Annnnyway, the result of this equation is that if you're a freshman just finishing your first semester chances are you're a victim of the "freshman 15." In other words you're pudgy and pasty from too much nervous binge eating, not enough sleep, and filling in the one meal a day not on the plan with a vending machine and bar snack diet. Remember fries and Coke are not basic food groups.

As with the rest of the Van Wilder Guide To Graduating College In Eight Years Or Less, it's not about getting through freshman year or even just surviving the college experience as a whole. It's about embracing life. And a big part of life is food! Learn to love your food and it will love you back (well, probably not the Tuesday mystery meat lasagna, it has a bad disposition and it's hard to get along with). But the deeper meaning here, Timmy, is that just because there are corporations putting double bacon Whopper Macs and Venti iced lattes in your face every four minutes, doesn't mean you don't have control over your own actions. Ask yourself, "Does a lemming have free will?" This also makes a great thesis for psychology 110 or marketing 280... You're welcome.

Speaking of corporations, you may be asking yourself "what about grocery shopping at 7-Eleven for the health conscious?" Well I'm glad you asked because you probably haven't given much thought about why you shop there at all, Sally. There are really only three reasons to do your grocery shopping at 7-Eleven: convenience, convenience, and high fructose corn syrup. High fructose corn syrup is everywhere at 7-Eleven. High fructose corn syrup is the main ingredient in everything from Sobe Elixir to Oh Boy! Oberto pickled sausages with cheese. At 7-Eleven you can even purchase water with high fructose corn syrup!

Once you get past the HFCS's you may also want to hum the following tune while you're shopping:

I love Sodium, beautiful Sodium,
but not just Sodium there's also Nitrates and
Nitrates of Sodium, Potassium, Sulphur Dioxide
and Sulphites, Benzoic Acid and Sodium Benzoate,
Sorbic Acid and Sorbates, Sodium Hydrogencarbonate,
Propyl Gallate, Tert-butyl Hydroquinone,
BHA and BHT too.

There's also Pectin, Lecithins, and Dextrins,
Potassium Dihydrogencitrate, Carageenan, Mannitol,
Silicates, Sodium Ferrocyanide,
and Iron Ammonium Citrate
to name just a few.

It's not like you shouldn't eat anything in the store, but it's like my old buddy Jimbo used to say: "Everything in moderation even moderation." Jimbo's not with us anymore though unfortunately – don't ask, it wasn't pretty.

*****

Read the packaging and do some research is all I'm saying.

*****

The silver lining here Sally is that this narrows your shopping list considerably. Here are your choices: Cliff Bars (certified organic), water (non-high fructose corn syrup), and Cheerios.

Case Studies To Consider

Grocery Shopping At 7-Eleven Case Study #1
6:00 a.m. — Returning from a downtown dance party and you're still rolling. Stay away from the candy isle and donuts! The ensuing sugar rush may leave you with severe brain damage. Pick up a pack of Dentine Ice and leave quickly. This is also the only time it is acceptable to consume Mentos (they're from Holland so it's cool).

Grocery Shopping At 7-Eleven Case Study #2
2:30 a.m. — After an intense afternoon and evening of study you went with friends to 2 for 1 pitcher night and forgot to eat dinner. Three words: DiGiorno rising crust pizza. O.k. that's four words, but you'll be hammered and you can't expect to remember that many words.

Grocery Shopping At 7-Eleven Case Study #3
4:20 p.m. — Munchies... must c-o-n-s-u-m-e chips. There are no healthy choices here, and your ability to discern them if there were any is gone. It's more about the texture anyway so go with Ruffles

---

7 Up All Natural?
In May 2006, the Center for Science in the Public Interest (CSPI) threatened to file a lawsuit against Cadbury Schweppes for labeling 7 Up as "All Natural"

Girls Are Smart:
Young women read food packaging labels at a 3 to 2 ratio as compared to their male counterparts.

brand potato chips and French onion dip from Frito-Lay. For an unexpected desert treat reach for the original Barnum's Animal Crackers by Nabisco... FUN!

Grocery Shopping At 7-Eleven Case Study #4

Anytime (totally sober) — If you're not picking up an emergency bottle of hydrogen peroxide, toilet paper, the morning paper, or coffee... see Cliff Bar and water above.

Other bonuses that come from grocery shopping at 7-Eleven include: the cashier will know many of the local cab drivers, they carry international calling cards, it's possible to make a beer run five minutes before the cut-off time, and there are interesting homeless people out front... see case study #1.

Things you May Want to Consider Before Entering The Store

- Why would anyone buy wine or sushi at 7-Eleven?
- Are microwave burrito wrappers on the floor of your car more incriminating than empty beer cans?
- Is Ramen food?

In the dorms, what did your refrigerator usually have in it?
"Freshmen year my refrigerator was constantly stocked with beer, cheap vodka and month old silk soy milk."
– *Kat Hirst, Senior in Speech and Hearing, University of Arizona*

F#@k Is The New Sh*t

It wasn't long ago that foul language was about non-existent in everyday discourse. B*tch… couldn't use it, cr*p… off limits, h*ll… only in rare cases, usually involving automotive repair or an embarrassingly painful experience. It seems like yesterday when using the word sh*t was a real shocker, but now even f#@k doesn't get anyone's attention, because it's becoming f#@king ordinary. Now it's not uncommon to experience people dropping f#@king f-bombs while ordering their morning latte and sh*t. Swearing is so f#@king universal that every other motherf#@ker has so much f#@ked up sh*t coming out of his mouth that it totally loses it's f#@king influence and that s#cks.

EVERYBODY'S DOING IT

******

Cursing is cool

******

That's right Timmy, curse words are your friends — but like your drugs you should never abuse them. Because where do you f#@king go if all of your best sh*t is passé and no one's f#@king hearing the emphasis? What's the next level? Are you going to use the c-bomb and alienate every female within twenty miles? Or are you going to resort to using the n-word? Come on, Timmy

VanWilderism #97
Ignorance is bliss, but knowledge is forever. Unless you develop Alzheimer's... then just f#@king forget about it.
Write that down.

that's so 1970's Richard Pryor to think that it has any play left. Everyone claims that word now: hip-hoppers, gangstas, Latinos, even suburban Asian kids. Its use is ubiquitous to just about anyone who knows how to slip it into conversation, with the possible exception of older Jewish stand-ups addressing obnoxious hecklers at the Laugh Factory – ask Michael Richards he'll f#@king tell you all about that sh*t my nigga.

In the future we'll have to resort to making up a whole new bullsh*t vocabulary just to compensate for the lack of f#@king effective sh*t to cuss with. Possibly the solution lies in a switch to f#@king foreign languages for those pendejos who can't come up with clever cursing in the f#@king English version of sh*t — merde!

Timmy, we're dealing with social norms here. It is ok, for instance, to hear swearing from musicians, athletes, and d*ckwad club bouncers, but it's still disturbing to hear it from politicians, business executives, and your f#@king mom. We'd all be a f#@kload better off if we used less of that sh*t and speak to people the way we wish to be f#@king spoken to. So keep the foul words in your back pocket until it's appropriate and you want to make a real impact. You'll appear to your audience to be more refined and intelligent, and when you do use it the results will be more effective. In other words: don't be an *sshole, leave the f#@king cursing to a f#@king professional, b*tch.

How do you feel about people who curse all the time?
"They're a f#@king idiot."
– *Jess Butler, PhD student in Sociology, USC*

Have you ever gotten in fights with other college students over rivalries?
"Yes... because it was $3 Jack n Coke night at the bar and no hot girls were there, and a fraternity-related comment was made... you can imagine the rest."
– *Jon Mccue, Senior in Neuroscience, UCLA*

Abstinence

Abstinence continued...

U. Decide:

When we asked if our respondents are sexually active, 66.5 percent said yes. Of that group though, 33.5 percent said they regret not waiting until marriage or until they found the right person before having sex.
U. Magazine

Sexual Congress:

A congressional staff analysis has found many American youngsters participating in federally funded abstinence-only programs have been taught false information such as, abortion can lead to sterility and suicide, that half the gay male teenagers in the United States have tested positive for the AIDS virus, and that touching a person's genitals "can result in pregnancy."
The Washington Post,
December 2, 2004

Abstinence continued...

✂

V-Card Pledge:
Columbia University researchers found that although teenagers who take "virginity pledges" may wait longer to initiate sexual activity, 88 percent eventually have premarital sex.

VanWilderism #39
Don't be a fool, wrap your tool. Because "always checking the turf before stepping onto the field," might have worked in your parent's day but with "flying V's" and "landing strips" it's hard to know what you're getting into now.
Write that down.

Tribes And Ego-centric Networks

While compiling the *Van Wilder Guide To Graduating College In Eight Years Or More* there have been times when I felt like a cultural anthropologist. Sally, you remember Jane Goodall, right? She was the woman who lived with chimpanzees in the Gombe Stream Chimpanzee Reserve of Tanzania to study their habits. In the sense that there are evolutionary traits similar in chimps and humans, she was not only a primatologist but also an anthropologist, or someone who is concerned with the study of all human beings at all times and with all dimensions of humanity. A cultural anthropologist on the other hand studies people in specific cultural situations, researching the way they function in society, their routines, religion, and entertainment, in short much like Jane Goodall a cultural anthropologist studies his subject's habits, which leads me to a conclusion...

******

We're all a bunch of monkeys.

******

You see, Sally, our collective college culture is like a big bubble bath. And in that big collegiate bubble bath we're all like little soap bubbles... little monkey soap bubbles. Each of our bubbles or spheres of friends and acquaintances represent the people we regularly interact with. Looked at in the macro the soap bubbles seem to intersect and overlap. Your bubble includes Timmy, me, your friend Tabitha, the guy from freshman dorm that hangs around like a sticky booger, but who you kind of like, because he always finds a way to make you laugh, some of Tabitha's friends, and a few others. While Timmy's bubble also consists of you, and me, in addition it includes a few mutual friends of yours, and an ex-girlfriend who you secretly despise. So it's similar but not the same bubble as the one you occupy.

People are creatures of habit, Sally. They take the same routes when they travel. They hang out with the same people. Listen to the same music. They form tribes that act like they do, *see Self-Guided Quiz Number Three – Diversity*. Which is all very normal but the problem is your bubble can become too cozy. You can become complacent and miss a big opportunity to open up to something larger than yourself and the close friends you've chosen to associate with.

******

Burst your own bubble.

******

Force yourself to take the road less traveled on occasion, just to see where it goes. Wear funky clothes and go somewhere you've never been, to see how it feels. If you want to really step out of the norm try some culture jamming. When you burst your own bubble and reach out to new people in unexpected ways you'll start bursting some of their bubbles too. It's a lot of fun. Like Jane says to her chimps, "Ohh, ohh, ohh! Ahh, ahh, ahh!" – Actually that's probably not a direct quote, but I'm sure if she did say it, she burst a few bubbles.

VanWilderism #17
One man's trash is a homeless man's lunch.
Write that down.

Dorms, Dating,
And Doing Your Laundry

Life is all about appearances. Shallow, I know but true. When you walk into a room the way it makes you feel is a function of several things, the décor, how it's organized, the colors, the lighting, and the smell. Sally, the place that you live in and how you choose to live in it is as important as your choice of wardrobe and cosmetics. It's also as important as the wardrobe and cosmetics you choose to borrow from your roommates. Appearances though are not just a display meant to impress others. It is often the appearance that you present to yourself that is most valid.

Look around you. Are you happy with how you're living? Do you have a professional setup in the place you study? It's called home "work" for a reason and work is for pros. Are your clothes comfy in the place you've provided them? Are they easily accessible and do you have a changing room or at least a full-length mirror that you can stand across the room from? Timmy, do you have an extra toothbrush around and a robe or oversized shirt for your girl?

Everyone assumes that being a college student automatically equates to being a slob, and I agree. But if there is a common thread that can be found in the practices that I have laid out for you it is this, be a bit unconventional and you will awaken parts of you that you might have gone your entire life ignorant of. Sally, resist the nest. Allow your space to be open and inviting. Like my good friend Johnny V. used to say, "Create a good space and it will be filled with goodness." Adopting this mentality really helped Johnny get through rehab. I think it can help you with your addiction to clutter too.

Timmy, embrace your inner metro-sexual. Get yourself a glue gun, a paintbrush, a hammer, and a staple gun. Pay a visit to the local thrift stores, and the fabric remnant outlet around the corner. You'll be surprised how sophisticated your place can look on the cheap. And if you're stuck for ideas... throw a party. Get your friends involved. I find my best decorating ideas come to me somewhere after the third shot of tequila anyway. Here are some pointers to get you started:

Animal-Free House:
A 1999 Harvard School of Public Health College Alcohol Study indicated that 32.3 percent of students living in substance-free residences drank heavily, compared to 52.6 percent in unrestricted housing.

- IKEA is not furniture. But it burns well at pep rally bonfires.
- The jet setter, rat pack, bee bop era is timeless.
- Throw out anything with Spiderman on it. I know it'll hurt but it's a right of passage we all must face.
- Books... you can buy used books by the pound and use them as support for your TV and PlayStation – it's ironic.
- Fuzzy + Funky = Fabulous (A word of warning, zebra, leopard, or tiger are best kept as accent and not as motif. It's the only thing Martha Stewart and Maxim agree on.)
- Indirect lighting = good
- Overhead lighting = bad
- Colored lights = good during holidays, and for Rico Suave impersonators.

Projecting a relaxed vibe that reflects your personality in the place you dwell will give you confidence and it'll make you happy when you're there. Having some scented candles on hand and making sure everything in your place can easily be thrown in the wash are also good ideas.

******

Ask For What You Want Because You Get What You Ask For.

******

I don't have much to say about dating. By the time you guys arrived at Coolidge you'd already been through the high school gossip mill, break up, phone call etiquette, heavy petting, and awkward sex rituals. But what I can say is no one is ever "out of your league." I'm not implying that you aren't the cutest couple on the planet. I'm thinking more about Taj and the time I introduced him to Naomi (that's I moan spelled backwards you know). She was hot, and he was... ummm let's say, scarred sh*tless.

Which was unfortunate because his fear made him uptight, and lead him to make some classic dating mistakes. He did learn some things though, massage oil will catch fire, and there is a fountain under his second story dorm room window. He also learned that confidence is sexy and you're only going to get that from experience. Fortunately college is a relatively safe environment for you to get some. No, I don't mean, "get some," Timmy, I'm talking "experience" like holding a decent conversation, getting to the gym often, trusting yourself, and developing a style that suits you. Regular haircuts help too. While you're getting some of that experience though you should set some guidelines. Here are some examples:

· Know when to say no.
· Know when to say yes.
· Know when to attend Lacrosse team parties.
· Know how to have a good time on ten dollars or less (you don't have to be cloistered just because it's the end of the month).

******

Your Laundry Knows Best

******

Doing laundry is not difficult, because your clothes come with built-in instructions. It's called a label. You should look into it. I know, I know, you were in a hurry, there was a lot to do and all your clothes were dirty, so you thought you could rush a couple of loads. The results: your whites are pink, your tees are covered with towel fuzz, and your wool cap looks like it came from Gap Kids. Slow down and get used to reading instructions. Detergents even come with instructions and there are usually instructions on the machines, and don't be afraid to take your best stuff to a professional.

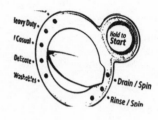

One last thing about doing your laundry, the dryer is the worst enemy of: rayon, polyester, nylon, one hundred percent cotton, and as in the previous example wool. That's why there are multiple settings. You can follow all of this laundering advice and keep your clothes looking sharp longer, or you can do like my buddy Craig does and wear only white and black. Craig's theory of laundry states, "two loads, bleach and no bleach." – I don't think it applies well to dating or dorms though.

VanWilderism #21
Luck is what happens when you've spent some time in the gym and the band is playing really loud.
Write that down.

Did you ever experience any laundry disasters?
"My experience with laundry was simply clothes not drying, but I remember my roommate's underwear being stolen numerous times."
– *Kat Hirst, Senior in Speech and Hearing, University of Arizona*

De Gustibus Nondisputandem Est

"In matters of taste there is no dispute." Timmy, Sally, I've spent a lot of ink describing how students tend to associate with their peers who act and look similar to the way they do, and I've spent an even greater quantity of pulp trying to persuade you to disassociate yourself from that behavior. You should still go with what you know, and you should feel comfortable most the time but on occasion look around you and try to appreciate someone else's tastes.

College is a big and wonderful melting pot of music, art, culture, and the performing arts. There are lectures and symposiums, foreign students, and debate societies. Not to mention a million opportunities for entertainment like live bands, dance parties, house parties, fraternity parties, and club parties seven days a week.

So my advice is: go out, enjoy, have fun, and be open to new possibilities. If you like a particular style of art, then that's your bag, don't let anyone tell you it's not valid. Unless it's creepy clown paintings, that sh*t weirds me out. Likewise if there's something that someone else is into then it's cool for them to like it. You shouldn't down them for it. De gustibus nondisputandem est, or paraphrased in English, there's no accounting for taste, especially when we're talking country music.

VanWilderism #109
Maury and Jerry do not make good study partners.
Write that down.

That Dare To Be Great Moment

As one door closes another opens. Timmy, you should be wrapping up the closing semester of your final senior year about now, and you're probably thinking, "what next?" We'll get to that in a moment but first let me share with you what Gwen wrote in the graduation issue of the Coolidge College Liberator.

******

"For four years I have been grooming myself for the real world. I, like many, define the real world as stuff that happens after graduation. But I was wrong. It took a man by the name of Van Wilder to teach me that.

You've all undoubtedly been to one of Van's parties. He's probably touched your life in some way, whether you know it or not. Watch Van do belly flops into a pool, but make sure you see he's raised $3000 to give the swim team a next season.

As you're all aware, Van was almost expelled. What you probably don't know is that he was set up by a pathetic, egomaniacal frat boy, one who this reporter knows firsthand to have a serious problem... with premature ejaculation. And in reaction to this lynching Van put in more effort in six days than most have all semester. Win or lose, we should thank him for reminding us what we're all capable of. That's simply what he does; he inspires the uninspired."

I always knew Richard Bag was a DIK but wow – premature EJ's that explains a lot doesn't it? Even with his stupid attempt at payback, facing the expulsion hearing was on me. I was responsible for that party, so what happened was my fault. Who knew twelve year-olds could throw back so much scotch… and Jäger?

My seven years at Coolidge taught me a lot. Let the record show that when I attended class I received exemplary marks. However it took Gwen to show me what I was doing… hiding. Maybe I was afraid of ending up like my father, whose whole life revolves around work. Perhaps instead of waiting for that dare-to-be-great moment, I just needed to open my eyes and embrace it. Because as Taj said, "If you do not see the potential in yourself, then you are a blind man. Go ahead and leave Coolidge, but leave the honorable way, as a graduate. You've been looking for that dare-to-be-great situation. It is at your doorstep."

Taj was right, Timmy, at least about graduating. He also said some stuff about sick boy, charities, a wet-behind-the-ears-kid from India, a woman's lotus patch, and masturbating in his father's woodshed. Taj gets carried away sometimes, but he's very inspirational. Like Taj I hope that I've been able to motivate you and Sally. Not to masturbate in your father's woodshed, but to embrace life's dare-to-be-great moments.

That's moments in the plural, Sally. You see I could have said, "enough, I've finally graduated, the world loves me, it owes me now, so I can sit on my ass and watch it grow fat." But I didn't do that because life is full of dare-to-be-great moments, not just the one. Life doesn't owe you anything after you graduate; you owe life.

******

Showing Up Is One Hundred And Ten Percent Successful.

******

Boomerang Kids:
Young adults who choose to move back home with their parents after a brief period of living on their own, usually at college. The phrase was coined during the period shortly after the financial bubble burst of 2000 that coincided with a more competitive global market of educated workers, which combined to make finding high paying jobs for recent graduates more difficult, and living at home rent-free more attractive.

We can all make a difference. Everything we do adds up to the sum total of our collective existence, good or bad. Don't wait for someone else to fix what's wrong with the world. Give everything you have to the things that matter to you. Even if you fail, do it spectacularly. Learn from your mistakes, be gracious when you succeed, and when you find yourself grumbling about life's misfortunes get up off the couch and do something about it.

So now, Sally, it is your turn to walk thru the graduation doorway and see it close behind you. As every commencement speaker pronounces, "You are the future!" And if after crossing that threshold you don't immediately find a door marked "dare-to-be-great," at least look for one posted "dare-to-be-employed." As Gwen said, win or lose I hope I've reminded you of what you're capable of... an entry level corporate job starting in the mid 30's, carrying crushing debt from student loans into the unforeseeable future, and little hope of ever claiming social security benefits.

Sally, there's one last thing that I want to impart. For finishing the *Van Wilder Guide To Graduating College In Eight Years Or More*, for following it's many tenets, and applying them to your college experience. I'd like to express to you, the words my father said to me at my graduation party, mind you he's only said this to me once in my entire life, "I'm proud of you."

VanWilderism #188
You know you're getting old when your drug of choice is Advil.
Write that down.

THIS IS IT

AN APPENDIX

A Wilder College Dictionary/Thesaurus

ABERZOMBIE (a bur zom bee), *n* **1.** a mindless tool who only shops at A&F. ("I can't believe that aberzombie, Tim, asked me out. He doesn't have a personal opinion on anything.") *See also: tool, moron, izodafarian, arrested fashion development syndrome, dork, popped collar, prep, preppie, prepster, khaki, cargo pant, cargo shirt, cargo shorts, Todd*

ALUMNI (aah lum nigh), *n* **1.** former students of a school or university. **2.** source of expensive presents for gifted collegiate athletes. ("There should be a rule against alumni coming to games shirtless to show off their body paint, it's getting embarrassing.") *See also: fanatic, donor, your future boss, old*

AUDIT (augh dit), *v* **1.** to attend a class without doing the assignments, or receiving a grade. ("Joey said he was going to audit Women's Studies 110 so he could ask the professor why there aren't men's studies too.") *See also: not failing, general waste of time, Joey's a goofball*

B.F.E. (bee eff ee), *n* **1.** a place that is far away from where you are. **2.** an acronym which stands for Butt F#@king Egypt. ("I want to drive, but I'm parked all the way over in B.F.E.") *See also: boondock, the sticks, the weeds, Timbuktu, in a land time forgot, east bumble f#@k, Arkansas*

BLUE CUPS – See **RED CUPS**.

BROKEBACK BOYFRIEND (brok bak boi frend), *n* **1.** a girl's boyfriend who is seemingly homosexual in every respect except for the fact that he's dating a girl.

("Don't tell me she's bringing her brokeback boyfriend with her. He's such a drag.")
See also: queerbait, closet caper, rainbow chaser, Tom Cruise

C U Next Tuesday (see u neh x toos dai), *adj* **1.** a euphemism for a derogatory term which refers to a woman's genitalia, used to describe someone who acts in an unpleasant manner. ("That librarian keeps hassling me over that Gettysburg book I lost. I wish she wasn't so much of a C U Next Tuesday.") *See also: minge, quim, muff, gash, axe wound, flesh butterfly, poonanny, box, bearded clam, fish taco, meat wallet, tampon socket*

DANK (da ng k), *adj* **1.** Originally referencing quality marijuana, more commonly used to describe anything of exceptional potency. ("Man, this new chicken sandwich is so dank, I could eat a hundred.") *See also: sick, chronic, awesome, cool, rad, crazy, tight, amazing, bombass, sticky icky, skunk, stoner logic, 420, Woody Harrelson*

DIP (dip), *v* **1.** to exit or leave. ("Everyone here is a douche, let's dip and go to my place.") *See also: bounce, exit, escape, peace out, scatter, vacate, run*

DROP (dr-aghp), *v* **1.** to cancel participation in a course, becoming the source of most upperclassmen's nightmares. ("When I was a kid I dreamt I was in class naked, now my dreams are filled with having to take McDougal's final without coming to class because I forgot to drop it.") *See also: not failing, audit, smart move, will a community college credit transfer?*

E = MC HAMMERED (ee ekwals em see hamurd) **1.** the equation that states if you get drunk enough you'll forget what happened, until you become that drunk again and remember it.

EMOROUPIES (ee mo rupees), *n* **1.** groupies for small emo bands no one's ever heard of, which are found only online, and typically having just a handful of loyal fans. ("Can you believe Stephanie is going to another PictureInPieces show? She's become such an emoroupie.") *See also: bandaid, roadie, chickehead, devotee, follower, fangirl, bottomfeeder, hanger-on, stalker*

FACEBOOK (fas book), *v* **1.** to befriend or contact someone online. ("I'm not sure of my plans yet, but I'll facebook you before the weekend.")

GEEBER (je ber), *n* **1.** a hit from a gravity bong, normally using a small amount of weed for one person. ("Let me take a geeber real quick and I'll be ready to go.") *See also: grav-hit, bong rip, toke, smoke, drag, hit, puff*

HELLA (he'la), *adverb* **1.** very much so. ("This party is hella lame. Let's leave.") *See also: really, very, uber, hecka, extremely, sweet, mucho, bazillion, gazillion, huge, Kirstie Alley's left butt check*

HIT (hit), *v* **1.** to contact. ("Just hit me sometime after work.") *See also: call, ring, text, e-mail, v-mail, holla, holla back, holla back girl, ain't no holla back girl, pointless and annoying lyrics*

HONDOLLAR BILL (hond daler bil), *n* **1.** an unattractive, loud imported car someone has invested too much money in, in exchange for no apparent gain. ("I don't want to ride with, Eric. He drives that ridiculous hondollar bill.") *See also: rice rocket, azn, fart cannon, pimpmobile, couscous rocket, POS car*

HOOK-UP (hook ep), *v* **1.** to engage in sexual activity with someone else. This can be anything from making-out to having intercourse. ("Yeah, I totally hooked-up with that blonde babe after you guys left.") *See also: make out, suck face, shack, shag, bash and dash, get with, one night stand, man-whore, pimp, slut, tart, skank, Professor McDougal's daughter*

ICE QUEEN (is kween), *n* **1.** a beautiful girl who is cold as ice inside. ("I took Mary out for dinner, but unfortunately she turned out to be an ice queen.") *See also: drama ho, sympathy maven, heartless bitch, varsity cheerleader, my ex-girlfriend*

IGNORASSHOLE (igner ass hol), *n* **1.** a person who is both ignorant and completely obnoxious. ("That ignorasshole professor ridiculed my project before I even had the chance to explain my thesis.") *See also: ignorant, asshole, jerk, jag-off, unedumacated politician, parking cop, concert security guard, your dad*

JONES (jonz), *v* **1.** to desire or fixate. ("Wow, I am really jonesing for some KK doughnuts right now.") *See also: want, desire, need, fix, Delirium Tremens, Courtney Love*

KANGAROO (ka ng geroo), *n* **1.** a woman with a small chest and upper body, but large rear and thighs. Often looks like a kangaroo. ("Julia's too much of a kangaroo for me. Nice rear, but I need some boobage up there.") *See also: marsupial, t-rex, sour-glass figure, your mom*

LUCKY (luk ee), *n* **1.** the first cigarette in a pack which is removed, flipped and put back in the pack to be smoked last. ("You can have a smoke, just don't take my lucky.")

MOCKCHICKEN (mak chi ken), *n* **1.** a chicken sandwich that cost only a dollar. ("I'm low on dough. Let's cruise over to the golden arches and grab us some mockchickens.") *See also: dollar meal, heart attack, stoner's surprise, munchie, pattyburger, bad idea, dripping anus*

NARC (nark), *n* **1.** any student who acts like a police informer. ("Don't let John come next time, he acts like such a narc.") *See also: informant, creep, sketchball, fed, tattle tale, squealer, dicktective*

NOMENCLATURE (no men clay tur), *n* **1.** a system of names perversely assigned to objects and ideas so as to confuse laymen in a particular field of study. ("We assign purposely obtuse nomenclature because, if everyone understood what we were talking about, there would be no need for experts.") *See also: WTF*

NOOB (n00b), *n* **1.** a beginner, or someone new and inexperienced. ("I don't want Andy as my racquetball partner. He's such a noob.") *See also: n00b, newbie, nublet, amateur, proletarian, dimwit, freshman*

OFF DA HOOK (af da huk), *adj.* **1.** exceptionally enjoyable or surprising. ("Did you see that Bowl game last night? It was off da hook!") *See also: hot, dope (antiquated), gangsta, wicked, fly, awesome, off the charts, da bomb, wigga speak*

PDA (pee dee ay), *acronym* **1.** when a couple's kissing is unpleasant enough to disrupt others. Acronym for Public Display of Affection. ("God, that's entirely way too much PDA for the cafeteria. I think I'm going to be sick.") *See also: pretty disgusting affection, airsnort, facesuckers, annoying*

P-FUNK (pee f ng k), *n* **1.** A Parliament Light Cigarette. ("Hey, man. Can I get one of those p-funks off you? I left mine in the car.") *See also: par light, cancer stick, cig, fag, cowboy killer, stogie, flashlight, red-light, neon-light, everybody's gotta a little light – under the sun*

PIECE (pes), *n* **1.** a device used to smoke grass. ("Has anyone seen my piece? I need it for the Dead concert tonight.") *See also: bowl, bong, pipe, gb, Sherlock, dugout, steamroller, one-hitter, burner*

PREREQUISITE (pree rek wi zit), *n* **1.** a condition that is required for a student to take a course. ("I'd be on track to take all of my junior classes if it weren't for all the prerequisites.") *See also: roadblocks to success, unpleasant phone conversations with the rents*

PROB (prab), *adverb* **1.** probably. ("I'll prob go. Haven't really thought about it yet.") *See also: prolly, thinks so, maybe, might, in all likelihood that event will transpire*

PWN'D (on'd), *adj.* **1.** to be defeated. Purposefully misspelling of "owned." Found in typing. ("Wow, you really got pwn'd on that picture comment.") *See also: owned, pwned, ownt, ownage, raped*

QUARTERLOAF (kworter lof), *v* **1.** an act of sexual deviance so disturbing it cannot be discussed. Always worse than what you think it might be. ("I can never go back into that classroom. I heard old Prof. Higgins and some senior citizen quaterloafed on his desk after mid-terms.")

RED CUPS (red kups), *n* **1.** drinks at a party. ("Watch out, I'm going to be sick. I think I had one too many red cups at that last party.") *See also: drink, beverage, beer, cocktail, mixed drink, junglejuice, alcohol, blue cups*

RENTS (ren ts), *n* **1.** parents. ("I wish we could go back to my place, but I live with the rents.") *See also: folks, mom an pops, parents, parentals, slave drivers, allowance bankers*

S.B.B. (es bee bee), *acronym* **1.** Slutty Big Boobs – Girls who think they're attractive simply because they have a large bust. ("I wish this girl would get off my nuts. She's such an S.B.B. and she doesn't even know it.") *See also: gross, brute butch boulderholder, big gal, big and bitten, vampire effect, boobs with boobs*

SCHWASTED (sh wastid), *adj* **1.** totally wasted. ("Dude, I was so totally schwasted last night I slept in the hallway.") *See also: drunk, hammered, stoned, high as kite, smashed, trashed, f#@ked, shitfaced, wrecked, gone, blasted, sloshed, inebriated, plastered, tanked, blazed, faded, you*

SHAME (sh am), *v* **1.** to graffiti one's body while they're unconscious. ("After Ben passed out from those shots, he got shamed bad by someone's sharpie.") *See also: deface, mark, f#@k-with, graffiti, tag*

SKETCHY/SKETCHBALL (ske ch e), *adj* **1.** someone acting particularly suspicious. ("Why do you always bring your roommate with you when you know we all hate him. He's such a sketchball.") *See also: unreliable, shady, unsafe, spaz*

SKEET (sket), *v* **1.** to blow one's load from enjoyment, literally or metaphorically. ("When I saw I aced that test I nearly skeeted all over my teacher's face.") *See also: splooge, cum, jizz, ejaculate, nut, jism, money shot, baby batter, payload, bukkake, Lil Jon*

SYLLABUS (sill a bus), *n* **1.** a summary of stuff you need to learn in order to pass a class. ("When's that paper due again? I lost my syllabus again and I'm completely clueless without it.") *See also: the bottom of your bookbag*

TENURE (tin yur), *n* **1.** the position of faculty or administration having a secure appointment until retirement. ("I can publish anything I wish, no matter how ridiculous or inflammatory because I have tenure.") *See also: pompous, arrogant, boring, windbag*

TIG BIGGIES (tig biges), *n* **1.** large breast on a woman. ("Angela has got some tig biggies on her.") *See also: tits, melons, boobs, knockers, fun bags, hooters, chest, rack, breast, ta-tas, breasticles, mammaries, dirty pillows, jugs*

THETA (thay ta), *n* **1.** the eighth letter of the Greek alphabet, used as a variable in every course in college and in the naming of many fraternal organizations, in order to cause maximum confusion in the student body. ("Doctor, it appears that the patient has become disoriented and agitated. He spends all day facing the corner of his room mumbling the word theta over and over.") *See also: science, math, it's Greek to me*

UBER (oober), *prefix* **1.** extraordinarily sweet or awesome. "I'm uber-excited about meeting your hot cousin." *See also: very, super, really*

UNPROTECTED SLEEP (un pro tek tid slep), *n* **1.** not setting an alarm while napping between classes. ("Sorry I'm late. I was having some great unprotected sleep.") *See also: napping, dozing-off, cat-napping, sleeping, Sally*

V-CARD (vee kard), *n* **1.** a person's virginity. ("I heard big-headed Patrick finally lost his V-card last night. Think it's possible?") *See also: virginity, first time, cherry pop, abstinence, your girlfriend*

WHIPPED (wh-ipt), *adj* **1.** someone completely bound to his or her lover. ("Steve is staying in again tonight with his new girlfriend. He's so whipped it's disgusting.")

WEENIS (wee-nis), *n* **1.** a new gaming system someone cannot stop playing with. ("Would you quit playing with your weenis and come shoot hoops with us?") *See also: ps2, ps3, nintendo, xbox, sticks*

WORD (wurd), *exclamation* **1.** yes, I agree with you. (A: "Let's go buy some beer." B: "Word.") *See also: yes, true dat, correct, okay, fo'sho, duh*

XANGA (zane ga), *n* **1.** an online blog chronicling every single thing you do everyday from scratching your butt to blowing your nose. ("Can you believe Sarah and her stupid xanga? Like anyone reads that crap.") *See also: blog, livejournal, myspace*

YARD SALE (yard sal), *n* **1.** originally reffering to skiers and snowboarders. To trip and loose all of one's belongings. ("Hahaha. Did you see Jenny come down those stairs and totally have a yard sale?") *See also: trip, fall, eat-shit, faceplant, stumble*

ZACH MORRIS PHONE (zak moris fon), *n* **1.** a large and clunky out-of-date cell phone. ("I wish my mom would quit being so lame and get rid of that Zach Morris Phone. It's so embarrassing.") *See also: out of date, calculator caller, unsuave, this list in five years*

Drinking Games Appendix

The Four Fathers:
Founding Games of Drinking

Beer Pong: *(also known as Beirut or Scud)*

The game of Beer Pong has several variations and any or all can be used. The rules of the game depend on house rules. Whoever owns the house makes the rules.

The basic rules are that cups are set up in a pyramid formation on opposite sides of an 8-foot table/piece of plywood/broken door, etc. There are usually four players on two teams, but it can be singles or a handicap match. The object is to toss the ball into the opposing player's cups, and the opposing team has to drink the contents of the cup. If any cups are knocked over they are out of play. Once one team has removed all the cups, they win.

The variations of the rules are exponential, but the more common rules include:

The Bounce Shot: You may bounce the ball while shooting, and if it goes in, the opposing team must remove two cups. But when you bounce, the opposing team can hit the ball away.

Balls Back: If a team makes both of their balls in one turn, they get the balls back and shoot again.

Bitch Blow: When shooting, the ball sometimes spins around the edge or the rim of the cup and if this happens the opposing team can blow it out before it hits the beer. (This is frowned upon in some circles or merely limited to "girls only" blowing.)

Money Cup: During set up, teams may decide to make a money cup. This cup will be filled to the top with beer, and if someone makes it in the money cup, the shooters can choose the drinker from the apposing team and that player must pound it in less than a minute or they lose.

A cup's a cup: No matter what the circumstance, if a ball makes it into a cup, the cup is gone. (i.e. If a player drops it into their cup on accident, a bounce shot is deflected into a cup, ball goes off the wall or ceiling, or just about any fluke coincidence with the ball going into a cup.

Prison rule: If you shoot the ball and it bounces back towards you and the middle of the table then passes the middle, it's anyone's ball.

Flip Cup (Tip Cup)

Two teams stand on opposite sides of a table, facing one another. In front of each teammate is a cup filled with beer equal to that of your opponent across the table from you. The first member of each team drinks his or her beverage. When finished, the cup is placed right side up at the edge of the table, and the person who drank it tries to flip it upside down onto the table using their two fingers. If they are not successful on the first try, the cup must be reset and re-flipped. Only after the first teammate is done flipping the cup upside-down successfully can the next person proceed. Whichever team finishes drinking and flipping all its cups first is the winner.

Sink the Ship

Fill a pitcher with beer and place a glass in the middle so that it floats. Players circle around the pitcher and one by one, clockwise, pouring their own beer into the glass. Players can pour as little as they want. At least one drop is required. One by one, players continue pouring beer into the floating glass until it's too heavy, and sinks into the pitcher. The last player to add beer must remove the submerged glass and chug it immediately.

Goon of Fortune

This one is from our Australian friends. Place a goon (Australian for "bag of wine") on a Hills Hoist, or if you're in the states, a Lazy-Susan will work. Similar to spin the bottle, one by one players spin the bag-o-wine while others chant, "Goon... Of... Fortune!" until the bag stops. Whomever the bag's nozzle is pointing toward when the bag stops spinning must squeeze the bag's contents into their mouth for at least ten seconds. Leaving to urinate, vomiting, passing on the drink, or passing out disqualifies the player.

Deal Me In:
Games Using Cards

Kings

One of the best drinking games, this game is great for crowds, boys and girls alike. Place a large mug in the center of the table and surround its perimeter with a deck of cards laid face down, making a complete circle. Players take turns drawing cards from the stack, each one with its own attributes. When drawing a card, the player must immediately flip it over so everyone can see the card revealed at the same time.

2. You. (Whoever you want must drink.)

3. Me. (You must drink.)

4. Floor. (or Whores)(All players must touch table or floor. Last to do so drinks.)

5. Guys. (or Social, everyone drinks)

6. Chicks. (Or Dicks)

7. Heaven. (Opposite of floor, last with their hands in the air drinks.)

8. Straight. (Or Drinking mate, you choose someone and they drink every time you do) (Card puller assigns drink to player straight across table from them.)

9. Bust-a-Rhyme. (Player starts a one-line rap that other players must continue rhyming with until someone breaks rhyme and is forced to drink.)

10. Categories. (Or Waterfall, see below) (Player picks category, *i.e. Types of Beer* then going clockwise, players name types of beer until someone repeats one or can not think of one and is forced to drink.)

J. Never-have-I-Ever. (Players hold up three fingers and go around listing things they've potentially never done. If you have done what is being said you take a drink and put down a finger. First person with all three fingers down ends the round and drinks again.)

Q. Questions. (Player can ask anyone a question. The person asked must then turnaround and ask someone else a question. You cannot ask the person that just asked you a question a question. Continues until someone messes up and answers question or cannot think of one.)

K. King's Cup (Player pours some of their drink into King's Cup, which is the mug at center of table. Mixing drinks is encouraged. The player to draw the last King must pour into cup, and then drink all of its contents.)

A. Waterfall (Or rule, a player may make a rule that has to be followed throughout the game. i.e. every time you cuss you have to drink, thumbmaster, etc.).

(Players all stand. Player that drew Ace starts drinking, followed by everyone else. Players cannot stop drinking until the player to their right quits drinking, starting with the player that drew the card.)

Asshole

Deal out entire deck to 4 players. Object of the game is to use all your cards first. Player with the lowest 3 card plays first.

Suits go spades, clubs, diamonds, hearts, with hearts being the strongest.

First person can play anything they like, a single, pair, triple, four of a kind, or a straight with at least three cards in it. The next person must beat this. If a single is played, a higher single will beat it, a straight, or a pair, three of a kind or four. You keep playing around the circle until no one can play off the card, or if you are unable to play you can put down a two in order to clear the board and play anything you want. First person to use all their cards is president, second is vice president, third is secretary, and fourth is asshole.

Once a hand is completed the president can tell anyone to drink at any time, vice president can tell his subordinates, and secretary can tell the asshole. The Asshole is also responsible for getting fresh beers, shuffling and dealing, and basically being the bitch for the current hand.

**Asshole has the right to make anyone drink during his shuffle and deal. Once deal is complete regular rules apply.

Up the River, Down the River

Set up one row for every player, five cards long. Players try to guess the properties of the card before it is flipped. In the first round, players guess red or black. Second is higher or lower than the player's first card. Third round is inside or outside of the first two cards. In the fourth round, guess the suit. Lastly players guess if their next card is odd, even, or picture. The player with the best five-card poker hand assigns another to down a full beer. The remaining cards are arranged face down in two rows and six columns. The top row is the "give" pile, the bottom is the "take" pile. Cards are turned over one at a time. Anyone with a card matching one flipped will give or take the appropriate number of seconds of drinking based on the columns. The first is two seconds, the next four, and so on until the last one, which is a full beer. If a player has a pair or three of a kind in their hand, the drinking time doubles or triples accordingly. If a card is flipped that no one has a match for, the top remaining card in the deck is used until there is a match.

Horserace

The most exciting speaker should act as the announcer, and a nimble-handed partner should handle the horses. Take the four Aces out of the deck and line them up at the end of the table, these will act as the horses. Lay 8-15 more cards face-down, in a single file line leading away from the lined up "horses." The remaining cards go into the announcer's hand. Everyone watching wagers drinks on their favorite horse, or suit. If someone wagers more than 10 drinks, they must drink half of them before the race begins to stop insane bets. The announcer lays down the cards face-up as quickly as possible, calling out the suits. The nimble-handed one should advance the horse matching the suit the announcer called out one card at a time. The first "horse" to make it to end of the 8 or 15 card line is the winner. Winners dish out the drinks they wagered, while the losers drink their wagers plus the drinks they're assigned.

World's Fastest Man: Games of Speed Consumption

Power Hour

Each player takes a shot of beer every minute for an hour. Another form of this game is called "Century Club." The rules are the same, players just drink for 100 minutes instead of 60.

Case Race

Each team is assigned a case. All cans must be completely emptied. Any team member that vomits, forfeits the game for their team.

Edward Forty Hands

Also known as "80oz to Freedom" this game involves players taping a 40oz to each hand. The challenge is not only finishing both bottles, but also using the bathroom, answering their cell phone, and lighting cigarette. They cannot be helped; they must finish the drinks if they want to use their hands.

Beer Bonging & Shotgunning

The object of both shotgunning and beer bonging is to consume all the alcohol as quickly as possible, without spilling any liquid. In preparation for beer bonging, players often let the air out the bottom of the funnel so the beer comes to the end of the tube. Shotgunning, or doing a "sub," has the same purpose as bonging. Participants poke a hole in the bottom of the can, and place their mouth to the hole. Popping the tab at the top of the can creates a change in pressure that forces the beer out the hole. Both are considered two of the quickest ways to consume alcohol.

Warning, Drinking Builds Brain Cells: Memory and Skill Games

21

Players sit in a circle. One player calls the direction of play by saying, "To my left" or "To my right." That player will then also say a number, or string of numbers, starting with one. The choice of numbers will dictate the direction of the game. Saying one number will cause the game to go to the next player in line (in the direction initially declared). Two numbers will reverse the direction of the game. Three numbers will continue the game in the original direction but will skip one player.

The onus of calling out the next number in the sequence will pass according to the string of numbers declared by the preceding player.

An initial call of "To my left, one," will mean that the player to the immediate left of the starter must say the next number, which in this case is "two." Alternatively, a call of "To my left, one, two," will mean that the player to the immediate right of the starter must say the next number, which in this case is "three." Finally, a call of "To my left, one, two, three," will mean that the player to the left but one over must say the next number, which in this case is "four."

The player with the onus of calling the next number has the same option; he may call one, two or three numbers. The direction of play will chop and change accordingly. The one exception to this is the restriction on calling two numbers following a two-number call. This is referred to as "doubling a double," and in some versions of the game is prohibited so as to make sure that play does not get stuck between two players.

The object of the game is to ensure the sequence continues to number 21 - the group objective. At the same time players will not wish to be the one to say 21 and be liable to consume their entire beverage, so skillful use of the numbers will be required to direct the play away from themselves.

Bullshit

This game requires a minimum of four players. Each player chooses a kind of shit to represent him, (i.e. "dog shit," "monkey shit," "dumb shit," "no shit," "green shit"). Play begins with the first player announcing, "Somebody shit in the parlor!" All the other players respond by asking, "Who shit?" The first player then accuses another player, calling them by their designated shit. The accused responds by saying, "Bullshit!" Once again, the other players respond by asking, "Who shit?" The accused then accuses a third player and so on. This continues until a player makes a mistake by calling out a non-existent shit, playing out of turn, passing play back to their accuser, or breaking the rhythm of the game. This player must then drink an agreed upon measure of an alcoholic beverage. After drinking, the player who made the mistake restarts play by announcing, "Somebody shit in the parlor," and play commences as before.

Zoom, Schwartz, and Profigliano

This game involves passing "energy" through hand motions and words. Players stand or sit in a circle facing one another.

Zoom!: Zoom is a direct pass. The passer must look directly in the eyes of whom he's passing to and say "Zoom." That player then catches it and passes to someone else. You cannot Zoom the player that just Zoom'd you.

Schwartz!: Schwartz is a pass back to who passed it to you. Looking them in the eye you say "Schwartz." Two players can Schwartz each other for as long as they wish.

Profigliano!: This is a fake pass. The player looks at someone else, and says/passes "Profigliano," but it actually goes back to the person that passed it to them.

When a player messes up, they are out.

You Got Change for a 40oz:
Games Involving Quarters

Quarters

Players each fill either their shot glass with liquor or mug with beer. Then they pair up and race to see who can bounce their quarter off the table and into their glass first. If done in a circle with more than one player, they start on opposite sides. Once quarter is made into glass, the quarter is passed to the player to their left. If one quarter catches up, and passes another, the person that skips them must spin the coin. Flicking the quarter sideways, they let it spin and try and stop it with one finger, still standing up. If they can do so, the player that was skipped must then place their glass upside down, and put another right-side-up on top of it. The player then has one shot to make it in the double tall glass or is forced to drink.

Land Mine

Players sit around a table with designated areas. These areas are about two beer can widths in size. Players spin their quarter from their designated area, and drink from their beer before the quarter stops. Players will accumulate empty beer cans they can use to "Land Mine" opponents. This happens after the player starts their spin and the player with the empty beer can slams his beer can over the top of the quarter. This makes a land mine, and makes the player who spun spin again. If the quarter goes off the table, they spin again, and if a quarter hits a can, the player drinks for each time it hits the can. The cans must be returned to their original position, so it's good to have a spotter. If a player hits a full beer on the table the owner of the beer must finish it, or if it's the spinner's beer they must finish it. The games progress until there is either no beer left, or one player is blocked in completely and has no way of getting out. They must then finish their beer, and dive through all the land mines clearing the table.

Robopound

Thank the boys at Princeton for this one. Two teams of four players, each forming a line on opposite sides of a waist-high table, and eight cups partially filled with beer are arranged in two staggered lines in the middle of the table. one player on each team is designated as the "first shot." This player must be on one end of his or her team line. The player at the opposite end of the line is designated as the "first drink."

Shooting passes one way down the line, while drinking passes the other way. Once cups are hit, any player may "tighten" the remaining cups by moving them in to reform two staggered lines.

To start the game, the two first shots have a social that is not constrained by time pressure. One player tries to bounce his or her quarter into any of the cups. The other player is allowed the opportunity to do the same. If both players sink cups, those players drink the cup they hit, remove the quarter from the bottom, and repeat the social. If neither player hits a cup on the first shot, time-pressure gameplay begins, and the next teammate in the line on each side takes their respective quarter as quickly as possible and tries to hit a cup. Players are only allowed one attempt to shoot, not counting the social. If one player hits a cup and the other does not on the initial social, time-pressure gameplay begins, and the first drink must drink the cup with the quarter in it while the next player in line on the team that won the social takes a shot. Once the first drinker finishes the beer, he or she must get the quarter out of the cup as fast as possible and give it to the next shooter in line on his or her team, at which point that player may shoot.

Watch and Drink: TV/Movie Games

Family Guy

Every time the show cuts to an irrelevant flashback or sketch, take a shot.

The Big Lebowski

Drink a White Russian every time the Dude has one. Drink every time you hear, "Dude," "Fuck," or "Shut up, Donny."

State of the Union Address

Every time the president is interrupted by clapping, take a shot of beer.

Walker, Texas Ranger

Drink every time Walker hits a man. Chug a beer for every roundhouse and boot related fatality. Experts Only!

Take Me Out to the Ballgame:
Sports and Songs to Drink To

Baseball:

Players bet on what they believe the next pitch is going to be. There are three options: ball, strike, or contact (foul ball counts as contact, not strike). Guess incorrectly, and you drink. Players can make risky bets (i.e. "homeruns") on any pitch for whatever amount of drinks are determined in the wagering process.

Foosball:

The best drinking game ever has simple rules:
1. No spinning.
2. All balls hit in count.
3. Players from both sides drink after every point.
4. First to ten wins. No overtimes.
5. No touching of the other player's pole.
6. No leaning or shaking table.
7. In doubles, player switch sides after losing 5 points to opposing team.
8. Spinning serves are allowed, and if made in, count; even if ball never touched a player.
9. In two player game, a goalie shot counts as 2 points unless it's reflected off teammate.
10. House Rule of Choice

Roxanne:

Drink every time you hear "Roxanne." Chug after hearing "Red Light" until the next "Roxanne" is heard.

Thunderstruck:

Start drinking when you hear, "Thunder!" and continuously chug until you hear "Thunder!" again. Repeat until song is over.

The Latest Releases From
The National Lampoon Press

National Lampoon
Jokes, Jokes, Jokes
Collegiate Edition
Steve Ochs, Mason Brown
978-0977871-827 Price: $11.95 US

National Lampoon
The Saddam Dump
Saddam Hussein's Trial Blog
Scott Rubin, MoDMaN
978-0977871-858 Price: $14.95 US

National Lampoon Favorite
Cartoons Of The 21st Century
*National Lampoon Staff And
Contributors*
978-0977871-810 Price: $14.95 US

National Lampoon
Not Fit For Print
*National Lampoon Staff And
Contributors*
978-0977871-834 Price: $17.95 US

National Lampoon Help!
Scott Rubin
978-0978832-322 Price: $14.95 US

National LampoonVan Wilder
Guide to Graduating College
In Eight Years or More
*MoDMaN
And National Lampoon Contributor*
978-0978832-339 Price: $12.95 US

National Lampoon
Magazine Rack
*J. Naughton
MoDMaN, P. Cummin*
978-0977871-803 Price: $17.95 US

The 29th Anniversary of
National Lampoon's
Animal House
Chris Miller
978-0978832-346 Price: $12.95 US

National Lampoon
Road Trip USA
Harmon Leon
978-0978832-308 Price: $14.95 US

AMEX: NLN